Of God and Pelicans

Of God and Pelicans

A Theology of Reverence for Life

Jay B. McDaniel

WJKP
Westminster/John Knox Press
Louisville, Kentucky

Book design by Gene Harris

First edition

Published by Westminster/John Knox Press
Louisville, Kentucky

PRINTED IN THE UNITED STATES OF AMERICA

9 8 7 6 5 4 3 2 1

Library of Congress Cataloging-in-Publication-Data

McDaniel, Jay B. (Jay Byrd), 1949–
    Of God and pelicans : a theology of reverence for life / Jay B. McDaniel — 1st. ed.
        p.   cm.
    Bibliography: p.
    Includes index.
    ISBN 0-664-25076-9

    1. Nature—Religious aspects —Christianity. 2. Life. I. Title.
BT696.M33 1989
231.7—dc20   89-31882
                                                      CIP

Contents

Acknowledgments

I want to thank numerous people for making this work possible. Chief among them is John B. Cobb, Jr., who graciously agreed to write the foreword. My indebtedness to him will be apparent throughout the book. Whenever I talk with him or read something he has written, my own thoughts are stretched beyond what I thought were limits to my imagination. More than anyone else, John has convinced me that imaginative exploration of alternative ways of thinking, prompted by hopes for a more life-centered future, is itself one of the most joyous ways Christians can respond to Christ.

My appreciation also goes to Charles Birch. Though others in the environmental movement have used the phrase "life-centered," Charles was the first I encountered who used the phrase in a Christian context and encouraged others to do the same. He did it in the context of our joint service on the working committee of the Church and Society Sub-Unit of the World Council of Churches. Equally important, Charles wrote a book with John Cobb, *The Liberation of Life: From Cell to Community* (1981), which spelled out in much detail various aspects of a theology of biology and a life-centered ethic. Both his friendship and his work have been a great stimulus to my own thinking.

I am also grateful to the staff at the Meadowcreek Project in Fox, Arkansas, whose commitments to sustainable living and to environmental education have themselves been sources of much edification for me. The founders of the project, Wilson and David Orr, and the Meadowcreek staff have done much to help me realize that a concern for animal rights alone, important as it is, is insufficient: it must be complemented by a concern for the Earth and its ecosystems, and for the people, particularly rural people, whose lives so explicitly depend on the Earth.

Thanks also go to the staff at the World Council of Churches. Having thematized "justice, peace, and respect for the integrity of creation" as the primary ideals in terms of which Christians might live as we enter into a new century, the World Council invited its various committees, including the one on which Charles Birch and I have been members, to think carefully and deeply about what it means to "respect the integrity of creation." It was in the context of that reflection that I wrote the first two chapters of this book, both of which were discussed (albeit in my absence, during the birth of my first child) at a consultation at Glion, Switzerland, in 1987. I am grateful to the World Council for giving me the opportunity to work out my own thoughts on the ecological dimension of Christian theology, and I applaud its forward-looking emphasis on a life-centered ethic.

My indebtedness also extends to the Institute on Religion in an Age of Science, a nonprofit organization devoted to considerations of relations between religion and science. I am a member of this organization, and through its help I have come to take evolution as a challenge and opportunity for fresh Christian thinking. In this regard the writings of another of its members, Arthur Peacocke, have been particularly helpful to me as I have sought a scientifically adequate understanding of God; hence the prominent role Peacocke's thought plays in the first chapter. Moreover, the institute sponsors an annual workshop on Star Island, a beautiful island off the coast of New Hampshire. In 1987 the theme of the consultation was "gender bias in religion and science." I was invited to deliver a presentation on gender bias in religion, which gave me the opportunity to write chapter 4 and thus to think through the nature of a postpatriarchal Christianity. I am grateful to members of the institute for helpful comments on the first draft, which in turn led me to make modifications that made the chapter much better than it might have been.

Others, too, have offered helpful critiques of earlier drafts of chapters. Linell Cady, Sallie McFague, and Holmes Rolston III, offered excellent critiques of drafts of chapter 1; Charles Birch, Linell Cady, and Sallie McFague did the same for chapter 2; Bill Eakin reviewed the entire manuscript, offering particularly insightful comments on chapter 3; and Rita Nakashima Brock, Paula Cooey, Peg Falls-Corbitt, Nancy Howell, and Susan Thistlethwaite responded to early drafts of chapter 4. Michael Fox of the Humane Society of the United States also offered helpful suggestions concerning revision of the entire manuscript. With all these people, I could not have asked for friendlier, more enlightening assistance. A special word of thanks goes to Rita Brock, whose own pioneering work in feminist theology (1988) has helped me to see how powerful the metaphor of "Heart" can be for men and women alike.

I wish to thank Lewis Ford, the editor of *Process Studies,* who gave me permission to reprint in chapter 2 of this work a section of an article that appeared in his journal (McDaniel 1988). More than most other process thinkers, Lewis has used the word "lure" to name God's mode of activity in the world, thus emphasizing that the presence of God in our lives is a pull from ahead rather than a push from behind; this insight pervades my work. Thanks go also to Eugene Hargrove, editor of *Environmental Ethics,* who gave me permission to reprint several paragraphs of an article (McDaniel 1986) that appeared in his journal. In private conversation, Eugene was the first to apprise me of the philosophical differences between environmental ethics and animal rights, pointing me in directions for resolving them.

I want to thank the administration at Hendrix College, too, for making this book possible. Not only has it offered a supportive environment for scholarship and publication, it provided me with a sabbatical in the fall of 1988 to make final revisions on the manuscript. I am particularly grateful to John Churchill, Academic Dean of the College and a philosopher in his own right, both for encouraging me in numerous ways to develop my own thinking and for reminding me through his own constructive, Wittgensteinian perspective that I might be wrong. John has been particularly influential in helping me to understand the religious significance of the "suchness" (see chapter 3) of everyday realities.

I am also grateful to my colleagues in the departments of Religion and Philosophy at Hendrix, not least of whom is Cathy Goodwin, who, with the aid of student helpers such as Stephanie McKay, patiently saw me through draft after draft of materials with good cheer and administrative expertise. Cathy's patience and encouragement were complemented by that of my colleague in the Computer Services Department, Jerry Blackburn, who helped make the use of computer resources an educational experience in its own right.

Finally, more appreciation than words allow goes to my wife, Kathy. Kathy's care and encouragement were ever-present in the writing of this book. Her own intuitions are models of a life-centered orientation for me, and her ideas in numerous discussions over the years weave their way into this work on almost every page. I dedicate this book to Kathy.

Foreword

Not many years ago one could speak of the deafening silence of the church with respect to environmental issues. Somehow it had internalized the focus on the human in its separation from the rest of the created world even more strongly than had the Enlightenment culture generally. The church feared that attention to ecological issues would distract from that given to justice. But this has changed. The tension between issues of justice and ecological sustainability has not altogether disappeared, but most thoughtful Christians see that both are essential and that in fact neither is possible without the other. The Nairobi Conference of the World Council of Churches was, in this respect, a turning point.

There has continued to be an anthropocentric focus in the church's concern for the environment. It is the environment of human beings that is considered, and it is considered chiefly because it is indispensable for human life. Features of the environment that are not important for human beings are still neglected.

Nevertheless, a deeper change is also going on. The recognition of the importance and value of the whole of creation cuts against supposing that everything has importance and value only as it affects human beings. There is increasing acknowledgment that the other creatures with whom we share our planet have importance and value in their own right. The time is ripe to affirm this clearly and to deal with the issues it raises. To do so is to bring to view above all the human relation to other animals. Are we justified in imposing suffering on other animals for the sake of human benefit? If so, is there a limit to how much suffering it is right to impose for trivial human advantage?

As in the case of environmental issues generally, the church lags behind the general public. Issues of animal rights are discussed extensively in recent philosophy textbooks. Activists have forced political authorities to recognize the importance of the issue of animal rights and have gained attention from the popular media. Only the church remains silent.

A few exceptions can be noted. Stephen R. L. Clark and Andrew Linzey are among those who have tried to draw the church into this conversation. Jay McDaniel moves this discussion forward significantly. He sets it in the widest context of reflection about God and the world. Although he writes as a Christian, he draws on Buddhism and feminism, showing that what is needed by Christians is more than a new doctrine or ethical teaching. It is a new worldview and a new sensibility.

For those who have crossed the threshold to this new worldview and new sensibility, the long centuries of Christian indifference to animal suffering can only appear anomalous. How can those who believe that God has created all the animals, and loves all creatures, treat cruelty to other animals so casually? How can they have so long refused to discuss human responsibility to the other animals? It may not be many years before these questions will be as hard to answer as is that of how Christians could so long tolerate and even justify slavery.

Perhaps the next assembly of the World Council of Churches will do for animal rights what the Nairobi Assembly did for environmental issues generally. McDaniel has himself been working through World Council channels to make possible such a step. If the assembly takes this step, it will no doubt explain its position in a rhetoric different from McDaniel's. It is unlikely that the statements coming from such a meeting will be as far-reaching as those that McDaniel invites us to make. But in the context of a new situation in which the church has finally acknowledged that this is a topic it is required to address, McDaniel's lucid and powerful statement will continue to press the conversation forward.

This book should have been written long ago. Since it was not written then, we can be grateful to McDaniel for writing it now. Hundreds of millions of suffering animals cry out to the Christian community to pay attention and to care.

JOHN B. COBB, JR.

Introduction

Within each of us there is a yearning for wholeness. Sometimes the wholeness we seek is only for the moment, and its content will depend on the circumstances at hand. If we are hungry, wholeness means food; if we are abused, it means courage; if we are victims of self-doubt, it means self-esteem; if we are victims of self-preoccupation, it means self-forgetfulness; if we are dying, it means inner peace. The meanings we find in moments of wholeness may be provisional, but they are also salvific. We cannot live, or meaningfully die, without them. And they are tastes of an ultimate, more lasting wholeness—an ultimate peace—for which our hearts simultaneously yearn.

This ultimate wholeness is not for us alone. It is for all who live and suffer. We may not consciously conceive this ultimate wholeness; instead it can be but a vague yet compelling hope in the depths of our experience. Some of us may even deny that ultimate wholeness is possible at all, all the while yearning for it at a prereflective and preconscious level. If we do envision it, however, the particulars of our imaginative picture will depend on the social and historical traditions that influence us. A native American will imagine it in one way, a Hindu in still another, and a speculative cosmologist in a modern university in still another.

Those shaped by biblical traditions often envision this ultimate wholeness as a state of affairs in which peace, or shalom, is fully realized for all who struggle to survive. The peace at issue is not between people alone, important as that is. It is also between people and God, between people and the Earth, between people and other animals, and between other animals themselves. John Wesley, for example, hoped for a "general deliverance" in which each creature would be redeemed. As Wesley imagined it, "no rage will be found in any creature, no fierceness, no cruelty, or thirst for blood" (1988, 102). Animals will be compensated for what they once suffered·

"they shall enjoy happiness suited to their state, without alloy, without interruption, and without end" (1988, 103). Here Wesley was interpreting Paul's hope that the whole of creation now "groaning in travail" will be redeemed at the end of history (Rom. 8:22). But long before Paul, Isaiah expressed a similar hope most poetically. In a coming age, the author said,

> The wolf shall dwell with the lamb,
>   and the leopard shall lie down with the kid,
> and the calf and the lion and the fatling together,
>   and a little child shall lead them.
> The cow and the bear shall feed;
>   their young shall lie down together;
>   and the lion shall eat straw like the ox.
>
> Isaiah 11:6–9

Not all of us will assent to the specifics of Isaiah's vision. It is difficult for us to imagine an end to predator-prey relationships. Still, we can rightly share that empathy for life which stimulated the author to articulate the vision in the first place. Behind that empathy we can indeed discern divine inspiration. And we ought to share the desire for a renewal of creation that motivated Paul and Wesley as well. For at this stage in history the world desperately needs people who are sensitive to the groaning of creation and who seek a renewal of life on Earth. This renewal may not occur in a final resurrection, although, as I suggest in the first chapter of this book, such hopes need not be dismissed out of hand. At least it can occur in the foreseeable future on Earth itself if we cease exploiting creation so as to allow the powers of life, and God within life, to renew themselves. The world very much needs people who are, as I put it in this work, "life-centered" or "biocentric."

To be life-centered is to be respectful of both life and environment. As a way of looking at the world, biocentrism is an antidote to that human-centeredness that sees humans as the measure of all things and that believes humans, and humans alone, are worthy of our moral regard. Inasmuch as human beings are members of the family of terrestrial life, and perhaps even its most precious members, life-centeredness involves a deep and abiding commitment to their well-being. More particularly it requires a special, life-transforming commitment to the well-being of the hungry, the lost, the forgotten, and the victimized of history, those whom Jesus called "the least of these" (Matt. 25:40). In our time we are fortunate that liberation theologies from Africa, Asia, Latin America, and Oceania, and from minority perspectives in North America and Europe as well, have made this point so strongly. Those who seek to be life-centered must drink deeply from the wells of liberation theologies so that a life-centered orientation is not a mere luxury for the comfortable.

But a concern for people, important as it is, is by no means enough. To be life-centered is to live out of a sense of kinship with all life, not human life alone. It is to empathize with other living beings, too, and to recognize that the Earth is their home as well as our own. An inclusive life-centeredness is needed because "the least of these" now include animals subjected to cruel treatment in factory farms and scientific laboratories, endangered and extinct species whose habitats have been disrupted by direct and indirect exploitation, and the Earth itself, with its shrinking forests, eroded topsoils, encroaching deserts, contaminated waterways, polluted atmosphere, and depleted ozone layer.[1] Even as we learn from liberation theologies, the theme of liberation must be extended to include other living beings and the Earth. We must recognize, as African Christianity can teach us, that our neighbors are not only other people "rich people and poor . . . black people and white," but also "animals and trees . . . mountains and grass . . . all creatures on earth."[2] Indeed, we must realize that in terms of sheer numbers the vast majority of our neighbors are plants and other animals. To exclude them as we attempt to live out Christian love is to exclude more than ninety-nine percent of our neighbors.

The purpose of this book is to offer ideas that can stimulate the development of a life-centered Christianity.[3] Much of the discussion is centered on God, since God, for me, is the very Life, immanent within each living being, by which all beings are lured to live, and by which we are lured to care both for ourselves and for other living beings amid our respective struggles to survive with satisfaction relative to the situations at hand. But the book is not only about Life with an uppercase *L,* about God; it is also about life with a lowercase *l,* about pelicans, for example. In fact, the book has four subjects, four aims, corresponding to the four chapters of this work.

My first aim (chapter 1) is to present a credible and yet meaningful way in which Christians and others might envision a life-centered God in light of the violence we see in life on Earth. The philosopher John Hick has spoken of those for whom "the pain suffered in the animal kingdom beneath the human level has constituted the most baffling aspect of the problem of evil" (1988, 62). I would not have put it this way, for I do not think it helpful to conceive other animals as necessarily "beneath" humans, nor humans "beneath" them. We are equally loved by God. But I am one of the people of whom Hick is speaking. I too am troubled by this "most baffling aspect of the problem of evil." This is where pelicans enter, for I take the plight of the youngest of pelican broods as representative of the plight of all living beings who groan in travail under the weight of evolutionary violence. In the first chapter I develop a panentheistic understanding of God in order to illuminate God's relationship to pelicans and, by analogy, to all living beings.[4]

My second aim (chapter 2) is to develop the foundations and guidelines for a life-centered ethic. Here it is not wild pelicans that receive special attention but, rather, "domesticated" animals whom we manipulate for purposes of food, experimentation, and recreation, because, with a very few exceptions (see Linzey 1987), they have so often been ignored in traditional Christian ethics. I try to link a concern for individual animals whom we have forced into our communities with a concern for the stability, beauty, and integrity of ecosystems. My aim is to bring together two traditions in ethics that have sometimes been deemed irreconcilable: one emphasizing environmental ethics and the other animal rights. I suggest that Christians can affirm both.

My third aim (chapter 3) is to add to an understanding of Christian spirituality by identifying and discussing certain inward dispositions that can nourish and support a life-centered Christianity. Here I think Christians have much to learn from a variety of nontraditional sources: from native American religious traditions through African spiritualities to Asian traditions. In our pluralistic age, it seems to me both unnecessary and irresponsible for Christians to move toward life-centered perspectives without learning from other religious traditions. My case in point is Buddhism, from whose doctrine of Emptiness, I try to show, Christians have much to learn concerning a biocentric spirituality.

My final aim (chapter 4) is to present a more general theological context in which the ideas presented in the first three chapters can be appropriated by Christian communities. I call this context "post-patriarchal" because it is heavily influenced by feminist theologies.

The reader will rightly sense a shift in tone between the first three chapters and the fourth. In part the shift is from a preoccupation with the nonhuman sphere to a renewed interest in the human sphere, from pelicans back to people. Such a shift is necessary, I believe, lest people be forgotten and a life-centered Christianity lapse into ecological misanthropy. But in part the shift is from the absence of an explicit focus on feminism in the first part of the work to a sustained discussion of feminism at the end.

Why bring feminism into the picture?

First, and most obviously, a life-centered theology that neglects the oppression of women is not genuinely life-centered. Of course, any people who are oppressed must be heard from a life-centered perspective. But most Christian feminist theologies include a concern for others who are oppressed. One way to make sure the theme of *human* liberation is part of a life-centered Christianity is to make sure that one's life-centered orientation is feminist-influenced.

Second, feminist theologies have shown that there is a close connection between ways of thinking that objectify women and those that objectify other living beings. At least this has been the case among Western Christians and those influenced by Western Christian attitudes. Therefore, an elimination of anthropocentrism (human-centeredness) in Christianity can best occur, and is most likely to occur, through an elimination of androcentrism (male-centeredness). Christianity can and will evolve toward life-centeredness inasmuch as it evolves beyond patriarchy.

My third reason pertains to the relation between feminist theologies and process theology. In all four chapters I draw heavily from process perspectives. Though I think there need to be many different versions of a life-centered Christianity, including versions that serve as significant alternatives to my own, I nevertheless find process theology the most helpful theological framework available for articulating my own deepest intuitions concerning a life-centered Christianity. Still, I recognize that process theology has often seemed inaccessible and abstract to those with concrete ethical concerns for people. To my mind, it is only with the transformation of process theology by feminists, which is now occurring, that process theology itself can avoid its past abstractness and move into a new, creative phase where its relevance to human liberation becomes clear. Chapter 4 attempts to contribute to that movement.

This leads to an obvious question. How can men, without claiming to speak for women or from women's experience, nevertheless appropriate insights from feminism? I do not think men really know the answer to this yet. We know that we have much to learn from feminism, but we are not sure how to learn. Chapter 4 is my own attempt to learn from feminism by accepting the implicit call of most feminist theologies for men as well as women to develop postpatriarchal ways of thinking. Those ways of thinking are ultimately as beneficial to men as to women. They are also beneficial to other living beings and to the Earth. Such benefits, I believe, are the promise of a postpatriarchal, life-centered Christianity. The purpose of this book is to point to this promise, and perhaps to help realize it as well.

1

A Life-centered God

"If God watches the sparrow fall, God must do so from a very great distance" (Rolston 1987, 140). This observation is made by Holmes Rolston III, a North American environmental philosopher and Christian who wrestles with the fact that so many sentient creatures die violent and painful deaths before reaching maturity. How, he asks, is God related to such creatures and their suffering? Does God share in their suffering, or does God watch from a distance? Is God empathic, or cool and distant?

As a case in point, Rolston considers the plight of newborn white pelicans. Female pelicans generally lay two eggs, the second two days after the first. Because few parents can raise two young, "the earlier hatched chick, more aggressive in grabbing food from its parent's pouch, becomes progressively larger, attacking the smaller sibling" (1987, 138). The second chick—whom we will imagine as male—is often driven out of his nest by the first chick. His return to the nest is prevented by the parents, lest they accidentally adopt an alien chick and waste precious parental energy. Nine times out of ten, he thrashes about in search of food and then dies of abuse or starvation.

Rolston points out that this mode of parenting has been very successful from an evolutionary perspective. It has led to the survival of generations of white pelicans for almost thirty million years. The second chick is an insurance policy in case the first chick runs into trouble. He is a "backup chick." Neither the parents nor the first chick should be condemned for their behavior. Both are genetically conditioned to behave as they do, and they have little if any capacity for moral responsibility in relation to the second chick. The treatment of the hapless chick is a "subroutine in a larger evolutionary process," a means to the end of species continuation (1987, 140).

From the backup chick's own perspective, however, this evolutionary analysis misses something. The analysis presents him from the outside rather than the inside. Viewed externally, he is indeed a cog in the evolutionary process: a mere backup. But from the inside, in terms of his own point of view, he is a sentient creature who suffers pain and enjoys pleasure, and who desires his own well-being, however trivial that well-being might be compared to our standards. Of course, the second chick probably does not "view himself" in the sense of objectifying himself as an "I" or "me." Such self-objectification involves conceptual and linguistic skills he undoubtedly lacks, as do human infants. His experience is prereflective and, analogous to our own experience in sleep, preconscious. But his behavior certainly suggests (1) that at least in a preconscious way he is aware of his own body and the surrounding environment, which is to say that he is sentient, and (2) that he has needs of his own, including the need to survive with some degree of satisfaction relative to the situation at hand. As a creature with sentience and with subjective needs, he is more than an object in the evolutionary process. Like a newborn human infant who has not yet acquired language, but who nevertheless has a perspective of his or her own, the second chick is a subject for himself.

As cognitive ethologists such as Donald Griffin point out (1984, 133–153), the recognition of sentience and internal needs in nonhuman organisms with nervous systems is not mere human projection. It is a sound inference from biological evidence. Analysis shows that birds such as pelicans have the nervous systems and the biochemical endowments to enjoy pleasure, to suffer pain, and to have interests in avoiding pain and preferring pleasure. Moreover, evolution itself posits a continuity between human mentality and nonhuman psychic life. As Bernard Rollin explains, "given that evolutionary theory is at the cornerstone of all modern biology, and evolutionary theory postulates continuity of all life," it is unlikely "that a creature that has a nervous system displaying biochemical processes that in us regulate consciousness, or that withdraws from the same noxious stimuli as we do, or from other dangers, and that has sense organs, does not enjoy a mental life" (1981, 41). It is more likely that the creature *does* have some kind of mental life.

And here lies the problem, at least for the chick. Because the chick is the second or backup chick, his yearning for satisfaction is frustrated and his life ends in pain. While the chick's brief existence may serve larger evolutionary ends, this fact is of no consolation to him. From his perspective, his life matters for its own sake. He is an end in himself.

How about from God's perspective? From the divine point of view, does the pelican chick matter for his own sake? Does God envision him as an end in himself, or merely as a means to other ends? This is the question that Rolston raises and one that any Christian interested in the relation between God and nature must address. It is the question that serves as the point of departure for this work. My purpose in this chapter is to develop and articulate a way of thinking about God that might serve a theology of nature, which itself makes credible God's love for nature, including backup pelican chicks.

I. Universalizing Divine Love

Rolston's comment that God must watch falling sparrows "from a very great distance" suggests that for God individual organisms—at least nonhuman organisms—are not ends in themselves. God need not watch them from a close perspective, much less empathize with them, because they are parts of a much bigger picture: an unfolding and open-ended evolutionary process. The implication is that individual organisms are, after all, too small to be noticed and cared for by God.

But how large is a God for whom some individual organisms are too small? How much care and concern does this God have? How much heart? We know from human experience that love involves care for other subjects—at least other human subjects—as ends in themselves and not just means to other ends. And we also know those who say they love humankind in general but who cannot or do not love humans in particular, who lack that tenderness and concern for individuals on their own terms, and for their own sakes, that is essential to the fullness of love. Such people see the big picture at the expense of the parts, the forest at the expense of the trees. Similarly, would not a God who is so struck by the vastness of "his" creation, to use traditional patriarchal language for the time being, that "he" cannot attend to the concerns of particular creatures lack heart? Would not God's love, too, be lacking? I believe so.

Let us begin with the assumption, essential to Christianity, that there is a divine Consciousness immanent within, though also transcending, the universe, and whose nature is unlimited love. By *unlimited* love I mean two things. I mean love (1) that is universal in scope, inclusive of all creatures with sentience and needs, and (2) that is infinitely tender, desirous of the well-being of each sentient being for its own sake and cognizant of each being as an end in itself. To imagine such love as characteristic of God is by no means to limit God. What makes God "God," and hence so much larger than we, is that God's love is so much richer than our own. Limitless love is both universal and particularized. It is unsurpassably broad and, with respect to each creature, unsurpassably deep.

Though in this chapter I focus on animals, it is important to emphasize that divine love includes plants and inorganic realities such as mountains, rivers, stars, and wind. Christians rightly assume that the range of divine love is correlate with the range of beings who can be loved and that all beings are lovable. Of course, God cannot "love" mere objects or vacuous actualities, except perhaps as aesthetic objects to be appreciated from afar. However, as I propose in the following chapter, Christians need not assume that there are any vacuous actualities in the material realm. With primal traditions the world over, and informed by speculative insights from the new physics, Christians can assume that sentience—understood in this context as the capacity of energy events to feel influences, albeit unconsciously, from their submicroscopic environments—is itself characteristic of the submicroscopic energy of which mountains, rivers, stars, and wind consist. Christians can affirm that there is no sharp dichotomy between sentient and insentient matter and that so-called "dead" matter is simply less sentient—less alive—than "living" matter. This is to say that nothing is really dead and that God's love— indeed, God's empathy—extends even to mountains, rivers, stars, and wind, or at least to the momentary pulsations of unconscious and yet sentient energy of which these material forms are vast and dynamic expressions.

Still, it is with animals that certain kinds of moral questions become crucial. Amid their sentience, animals with advanced nervous systems, and hence with psyches, seem to possess *interests*—for example, in avoiding pain and enjoying pleasure—that we can and do violate in a way unparalleled in the inorganic arena. While it is not clear that in hewing stones we violate the interests of energy events within the stone, it is readily apparent that in slaughtering certain animals we violate their interests in surviving with some degree of satisfaction. As I suggest in the following chapter, all existents have an *intrinsic value* worthy of our respect, love, and preservation, but only individual animals can possess *moral rights*. As the example of the pelican chick makes clear, we live in a world in which these moral rights are largely unrecognized, persistently violated, and mutually conflicting. The first chick exercises a "right to survive" at the expense of the second chick. What kind of God would have created a world like this? It is because the pain of animals raises such serious questions for Christian faith that I focus on God's love for animals here.

To begin a theology of nature with the assumption that God is limitlessly loving, and that this limitless love involves empathy for animals, is to begin in an unusual way. Many theologies of nature start with the assumption that God is the Creator of nature and then ask how, in light of this fact, God might also be loving. Their assumption is that a Christian understanding of nature must begin with a doctrine of divine creativity. By contrast, I begin with the assumption that God is limitlessly loving and then ask how, in light of this fact, God might also be creative. My approach begins not with the idea that nature is utterly dependent on God but rather with the idea that nature, whether utterly dependent or partially independent, is inexhaustibly loved by God. If power is understood as the power to create out of nothing, I begin not with divine power but rather with divine pathos (Heschel 1965, 24).

I begin with the idea of divine love because I think this starting point best complements Christian spirituality at its deepest level. At its deepest, Christian worship is rooted not in fear of divine power or in awe of divine majesty, important as such dispositions might be, but rather in appreciation of, and in responsiveness to, divine love. To love God is to respect God, to care for God, to appreciate God, to be grateful to God, to empathize with God, and to want to be open to God. The image of God that best elicits respect, care, appreciation, gratitude, empathy, and openness is the image of God as all-loving. Other dispositions can enter into and enrich our piety—such as fear and awe—but these have their meaning only in the context of divine love. They should be supplementary rather than central to the heart of Christian piety and prayer, which is love for the God who loves.

To assume that God is all-loving is a matter of faith. As Christians most of us do not know with absolute certainty that the divine Consciousness is all-loving, but we feel and hope that it is like this, and we live by this hope. Another word for hope is "trust," and still another, "faith." We have faith in a God whom we trust is all-loving. Our trust is directly indebted to Judaism and to Jesus, at least as he was interpreted by various gospel writers and by subsequent generations of Christians. It is nourished by the idea—imperfectly transmitted through doctrines, rituals, and communities—that Jesus was, or sought to be, fully loving, and that to the degree he realized this ideal, he revealed God's nature. If we take the love that Jesus strove to embody, if we imaginatively extend its breadth and depth beyond limit, and if we then envision that breadth and depth as gathered into the unity of a single, universal Consciousness, we have an image of God. Whatever else it is, we trust that the divine Mystery is a wellspring of unlimited love.

Assuming that the divine Consciousness is Jesus-like, we cannot rest content with Rolston's suggestion that God watches falling sparrows and flailing pelicans "from a very great distance." Such a God would lack depth. Rather, we must try to understand how God's unlimited love extends even to the smallest of creatures, even to the "least of these," even to the second pelican. In developing our theologies of nature, then, we have three tasks.

Three Tasks for a Christian Theology of Nature

First, we must find some way of imagining God as inexhaustibly large-hearted: that is, as so completely empathic that God is inside the skin of each sparrow, each pelican, and each sentient creature, suffering its sufferings and enjoying its joys along with it. To do this we can follow the lead of those contemporary theologians who emphasize divine suffering. We can agree with Arthur Peacocke, for example, who insists that "any serious consideration of the creative action of God as dynamic and evolutionary is inexorably led to face the fact of death, pain, and suffering in that process and so come to an understanding of God as the *suffering* Creator" (1979, 200).

Second, inasmuch as we deem God a creator, we must find a way of imagining God's creativity such that, even if God is responsible for the fact that there is a world as we know it, God is not indictable for worldly suffering. Here we can follow the lead of process theologians and recognize (1) that God's power is, and always has been, persuasive or invitational rather than coercive, (2) that the natural world has creativity that is independent of God's creativity, and (3) that, by virtue of nature's creativity, patterns of behavior can emerge in the evolutionary process that even God could not and cannot prevent if there is to be life at all. To recognize that there are limits to divine power is to recognize that there are empirical as well as logical constraints on divine power. It is also to diverge from the dominant tradition of classical Christian theology. It is to say that God is all-loving but not all-powerful, as the latter has traditionally been understood. But perhaps it is to take even more seriously than the dominant tradition the revelatory implications of the cross of Jesus. It is to see that divine power itself is, and always has been, creatively vulnerable.

Third, we must find a way of articulating our hope that, while the suffering of creatures may not be preventable by God, this suffering is nevertheless redeemable by God. This is to hope that even though certain crosses are unavoidable, resurrection can occur.

In the following sections of this chapter, then, I will suggest a way of thinking about God in relation to nature which shows that God suffers with each particular sentient being; that God's creative activity is the most influential power in the universe, though nonetheless subject to certain limitations; and that though God's power is subject to limitation, it is nevertheless powerful enough to redeem. Before proceeding, it is appropriate to note the two resources that will serve as my primary guides.

Two Resources for a Theology of Nature:
Arthur Peacocke and Process Theology

A Christian theology of nature must involve more than a model of God. It must have a clear image of nature, with "nature" defined as a totality of finite existents that have existed in the past, that do exist in the present, and that may exist in the future. Today, of course, any theological understanding of nature must emerge out of an encounter with the methods and insights of the natural sciences. This is the case not only because science teaches us much about nature but because, in a contemporary setting, science much more than theology shapes human understandings of nature. In order to be credible, a theology of nature must be scientifically informed.

It is fortunate that today there are those within the Christian community who are doing excellent work in developing scientifically informed understandings of nature. Among those in the United States are such process theologians as Ian Barbour, John B. Cobb, Jr., and David Ray Griffin, plus, from Australia, Charles Birch. My own theological perspective is most deeply shaped by process theology, and one of the purposes of this book is to extend and advance the process tradition. Still, there are other theological perspectives that can contribute to a contemporary theology of nature. Among them is that of Arthur Peacocke from England, who has developed an impressive theology of nature of his own.

In what follows I will develop my own model of the divine reality by juxtaposing the process understanding of God with Peacocke's model. Let me begin, then, by highlighting three affirmations concerning "the nature of nature" that process theologians and Peacocke seem to share, albeit with different emphases and from different points of view. For it is nature as thus conceived into which the pelican finds itself thrown, and it is nature as thus conceived that must be the subject of God's love.

First, both Peacocke and process theologians affirm that human life in its psychological as well as its physical dimensions is an expression of, rather than an exception to, nature. Peacocke qualifies this a bit by suggesting that human self-consciousness may protrude "beyond the boundary of nature" (1984, 96). But his intention is not, I believe, to advocate a dualistic ontology in which the human mind is a substance different in kind from matter (1979, 122–125). Along with process thinkers, Peacocke eschews a dualistic ontology that posits two distinct realms of being: one natural and the other supernatural. For both, the visible worlds of space-time and the invisible worlds of thought and feeling are part of a single whole called "nature" or, to use the Jewish, Christian, and Muslim term, "creation."

Second, both insist that nature (including human life) is dynamic and evolutionary rather than static and unchanging. Both stress that the cosmos as we know it evolved to its present state, and is evolving even now into an as yet undetermined future. Both are open to the possibility that this cosmic epoch (beginning with the big bang ten to twenty billion years ago and ending either with a big chill or a heat death) may itself be but one of a beginningless and endless series of cosmic epochs. Both see life on Earth as a unique and distinctive part of this larger evolutionary process.

Third, both affirm that nature—matter itself—is in certain ways creative. This is to say that in various ways it is imbued with potentialities, the actualizations of which cannot be precisely predicted in advance, and that, at the biological level at least, evolution occurs as the result of chance (to be defined shortly) as well as law. At the subatomic level, Peacocke and process theologians both affirm the indeterminacy implied by quantum mechanics. At the molecular level and higher, both affirm the creativity of what the physical chemist Ilya Prigogine calls "dissipative structures." At the human level, both see the creativity of matter as taking the form of what we call freedom (Peacocke 1979, 57, 97–100).

In what follows, let us assume with Peacocke and process theologians that nature is indeed something that includes rather than excludes human life, that it is evolutionary and open-ended, and that matter itself is creative, unfolding in terms of chance as well as law.[1] And let us then ask, in light of this way of thinking about nature, how God might be envisioned as *loving* nature both in its vastness and its particularity.

II. The Receptivity of God

Here, too, Peacocke and process theologies can help. Both endorse the view that the universe is "in" God, even though God is more than, and not exhausted by, the universe. A word often used to name this perspective is panentheism, which means, literally, "all in God." It is from panentheistic perspectives, I believe, that Christians have most to learn in developing images of divine love for nature. However, there are two types of panentheism—emanationist and relational—and Christians must choose between them. Both types can be explained by using an analogy developed by Peacocke and by process theologians that draws upon our own experience of, and relation to, our bodies. The analogy is that God is to the world as a mind (with its mental states) is to its body. The world, according to the analogy, is God's body.

Emanationist panentheism sees God's body as a direct expression of God's own being, somewhat as photons emitted from the sun are expressions of the sun's own substance. To look at the God-universe relation this way is to believe (1) that the "stuff" of which the world consists is an expression of the very "stuff" that constitutes God's own existence, and (2) that the history of the universe, in generality and detail, is directly expressive of the will or purposes of God. By "stuff" in this context I mean the creativity inherent in matter, by which evolution itself is propelled. Emanationist panentheists view nature's creativity as God's creativity.

Relational panentheism, which I advocate along with other process theologians, and which to my mind is more biblical than emanationism, sees the world as having some degree of creative independence from God, somewhat as our own bodies, even though part of who and what we are, have some degree of independence from us as psyches. In biblical terms this independence belongs to the chaos from which, in Genesis, God called the world into existence, a chaos that, from the point of view of the biblical authors, probably existed along with God at the outset of creation (Peacocke 1979, 82). To look at the God-world relation in light of a relational panentheism is to believe that (1) the "stuff" of which the world consists is not identical to the "stuff" of which God consists, and (2) that the history of the universe, in generality and detail, is not always expressive of the will or purposes of God, though it may be. Whereas in emanationist panentheism there is ultimately only one creative power—namely, God—in relational panentheism there are multiple creative powers, of which God is the primordial but not exclusive instance.

Relational perspectives allow for a recognition of the receptivity of God. From the vantage point of lived experience, we are related to our bodies in at least two ways. We are *agents* with respect to our bodies, which is to say that we act in and through our bodies. And we are *patients* with respect to our bodies, which is to say that we, as psyches, feel the presence of our bodies and in so doing are affected by our bodies. An emanationist perspective can well offer an image of divine agency, because it equates the world's agencies with God's agency. But it has few resources to develop an image of divine patience, for, to receive something, that something must be "other" than oneself, with integrity of its own. In emanationist panentheism, the world is not other than God. God is not a patient.

In relational panentheism, on the other hand, the world is other than God even as it is in God. God is a patient who receives the world. Consider the fact that from a phenomenological perspective our bodies are in our experience: that is, in our bodily awareness in such an intimate way that we identify with them and speak of them as our own. Similarly, so the relational panentheist proposes, worldly creatures are in God's experience, in God's awareness as subjects with which God identifies as God's own. Just as, from a first-person point of view, what happens in and to our bodies happens in and to us, so the relational panentheist will say, what happens in and to the lives of creatures happens in and to God. In the case of God, of course, the awareness at issue is much more detailed and complete. Whereas we are aware of only a small fraction of what occurs in our own bodies, on this analogy God is aware of, and empathetically identified with, each and every event in the divine body: be it a pulsation of energy in the depths of a star, a moment of sentience in the life of a bacterium, a moment of pleasure in the life of a deer, or an occasion of joy in an exchange between friends. More even than our own bodies are present to our psyches, the world is present to God. Indeed, the world is immanent within, and present to, God, even as God is immanent within, and present to, the world.

The mind-body analogy helps us to understand how the world can have a life of its own even as it is immanent within God. Just as a fetus within a woman's body has a life of its own even though it is part of the woman, so the world has a life of its own even though it is part of God. Living cells in our bodies have sentience and creativity in their own right: creativity that, when functioning in coordinated fashion as organs and fetuses, can enrich our own psychic experience, but that, as we know from cancer and miscarriages, can diverge from our own psychic purposes. From a relational perspective, worldly creatures are like cells in the body of a divine Psyche. They are other than God even as they are within God.

To say that the world is immanent within God even as other than God is to say that God suffers. For Christians, this is one aspect of the truth of the cross. As Dorothee Soelle points out, it is an unspeakable shame that the truth of the cross has often been understood most deeply by many who have been victimized by the cross: that is, by Jews who for centuries have been wrongly identified as Christ-killers. In this context Soelle reminds us of Elie Wiesel's eyewitness account (1960, 70) of the suffering child at Auschwitz:

> The SS hung two Jewish men and a boy before the assembled inhabitants of the camp. The men died quickly but the death struggle of the boy lasted half an hour. "Where is God? Where is he?" a man behind me asked. As the body, after a long time, was still in agony on the rope, I heard the man cry again, "Where is God now?" And I heard a voice within me answer, "Here he is—he is hanging here on this gallows."

In this passage Wiesel speaks as one whose belief in God has been destroyed by an encounter with radical evil. His point is that, in light of the boy's suffering, there can be no omnipotent and omnibenevolent God. Yet his point can also illustrate the perspective of a relational panentheist. For the relational panentheist God was indeed in the boy, suffering with him, because he was in fact in God, as are we all. This does not mean that the boy's suffering was in any way justified, or that the boy suffered less because God shared in his pain. It does mean that God suffered more than God might otherwise have suffered, that what happens in the world can increase or decrease the pain of God.

As Christians learn to repent of our insensitivity to Jews and to God, we might also learn to repent of our insensitivity to the rest of creation, including, as I emphasize in this chapter, to other animals. I do not mean to imply that on a qualitative level the suffering of Jews, or any other humans for that matter, can be compared to that of nonhuman creatures. Nor do I mean to imply that I can fully comprehend the suffering of those who died in the Holocaust. I do mean to say that the suffering of an all-loving God need not be limited to humans. A God who suffers only with humans is too small. Our task is to recognize that there are countless crosses in our world, nonhuman as well as human, to which countless victims are involuntarily nailed, often by powers that have nothing to do with human agency. When as Christians we think of natural evil, we must include the countless instances of undesired suffering—which are "evil" from the creaturely victim's perspective—that are in no way the consequence of human sin. We must remember that God suffers from these evils as well.

But how intimate is this divine suffering with human and nonhuman life? Here the mind-body analogy has limitations. A pregnant woman may feel the effects of whatever pain a fetus might feel, but she does not really feel the pain as the fetus feels the pain. A man may feel the effects of damage to cells in his body, but he does not feel that damage as the cells themselves feel it. Here the analogy must be imaginatively amplified. If we are to imagine the suffering of God who is limitlessly loving, we must imagine it as perfect empathy: an empathy that feels the feelings of worldly subjects as the subjects themselves feel those feelings.

Divine Empathy

Three points need to be made about perfect empathy. First, it involves sympathetic understanding of the "inner perspective" of individual living beings. It does not watch creatures from afar, observing their behavior as from a distance; it feels creatures from their own point of view: that is, from a point of view that overlaps and coindwells their own perspective. As John Cobb argues, God can be conceived as both omnispatial and nonspatial, as "everywhere" and "nowhere" (1969, 77–86). Inasmuch as God is omnispatial, God is "within" the bodies of embodied creatures, human and nonhuman, experiencing the world from their own spatiotemporal perspectives and, as perfectly empathic, sharing in their psychic states. This means that as we humans watch a starving pelican chick, we are watching God. For God is actually there, in the chick, suffering with it. Even as worldly creatures are immanent within God, God is immanent within them.

To say that God is immanent within creatures is to say that God is present in their lives and experiences. This immanence can take one or both of two forms. God may be immanent as an agent, in some way guiding or directing creaturely activities, or God may be immanent as a patient, feeling creatures' feelings and experiencing along with them. In this work I endorse both forms of immanence, proposing in the section that follows that God is immanent as an active lure, beckoning creatures toward life and wholeness. At issue in discussing divine empathy, however, is the immanence of God as a patient. As a receptive subject, God takes the form of what the Jewish tradition sometimes calls the Shekinah, the indwelling presence of God in the world. As Soelle explains, "according to cabalistic teaching God does not forsake the suffering world"; rather (and here she quotes Martin Buber), God "descends to the world, enters into it, into 'exile,' dwells with the troubled, the suffering creatures in the midst of their uncleanness—desiring to redeem them" (Soelle 1975, 145–146; Buber 1960, 101). As Shekinah, Soelle tells us, God is a cosufferer "hanging on the gallows at Auschwitz" (1975, 146).

The second point to make about perfect empathy—implied by Buber's suggestion that the divine Shekinah desires that creatures be redeemed—is that it includes a sense of lamentation and a yearning for things to be different. If God's empathy is anything like our own, albeit infinitely more sensitive and tender, this empathy must be complemented by evaluation. When we empathize with another person who is suffering, we not only feel the feelings of the person, we also evaluate those feelings in light of what we take to be the best interests of the person at issue. If the person is suffering from a severe depression, we feel his or her feelings, and we do so in light of our own conviction that he or she would be "better off" if this state of mind were otherwise. Analogously, if we are to assume that God feels the feelings of suffering chicks, we must also imagine that God wishes that the "best interests" of the chick could be realized, whatever those best interests are.

It is possible, of course, that the best interests of the second pelican chick are to die of starvation for a greater, evolutionary cause. In this case God would feel the feelings of the suffering chick and be pleased! But this understanding of the chick's best interests is certainly alien to the chick's own point of view. From the chick's own perspective, his own "best interests," at least penultimately, are to survive with some degree of satisfaction relative to the situation at hand. He does not choose this interest in surviving, as if he might have chosen otherwise. Rather he, like most living beings, has a natural will to live. Given the inescapability of this impulse, I would imagine that God would appreciate rather than reject the chick's own interests. God, too, must wish the satisfaction of the chick and, in God's own way, be saddened rather than pleased. In the evaluative aspect of divine empathy, there must indeed be much lamentation.

The third point to make about perfect empathy is that it is one aspect—and perhaps an often neglected aspect—of divine knowledge. In its sympathy for the internal perspective of a creature on its own terms, and in its evaluation of that creature's conditions in light of its own best interest, God "knows" a creature. This is not knowing about the creature; it is knowing with the creature. It is a knowledge that is care. In Whitehead's words, God is a "fellow sufferer who *understands*" (1978, 351, emphasis mine).

This discussion of divine empathy raises an obvious set of questions. If much of life is lamentable, even to God, why are things not otherwise? If God is an agent who creates and sustains the world, why is there so much undesired pain? How, after all, does God act?

III. The Agency of God

In an excellent anthology of essays called *God's Activity in the World: The Contemporary Problem,* the editor, Owen Thomas, explains the importance of these questions. "At the heart of Christian faith," he says, "is the affirmation that God is present and active in the creation to carry out the divine purposes and to achieve the divine goal of fulfillment of all creatures" (1983, 1). And yet, as Thomas explains, "the development of modern science in the seventeenth and eighteenth centuries with its sole concern with natural causes and its ever-expanding interpretation of natural events led to fundamental doubts about the reality of divine activity in the world" (1983, 3). There has been a serious gap between liturgical proclamations that God acts in the world to fulfill all creatures and theological suggestions concerning how, after all, this activity occurs. Thomas' anthology shows that there are several possible contemporary responses to this lacuna.[2] Here I cannot survey all the approaches. Instead I will focus on the ways of thinking about divine agency developed by process thinkers and Peacocke, each of which draws upon the mind-body analogy.

Given the mind-body analogy, at least two types of agency are conceivable for God: unilateral or invitational. Unilateral agency is coercive or manipulative. It is agency that can infallibly effect its intentions to produce a desired state of affairs because the agent is in complete control over the objects that must be influenced in order for that state of affairs to occur. We feel that we have unilateral control over our arms, for example, because when we internally choose to raise our arm, our arm rises as the apparently inevitable outcome of our intentions.

Invitational agency is persuasive rather than coercive, relational rather than unilateral. It is agency that cannot infallibly effect its intentions to produce a desired state of affairs because the agent requires the cooperation, and perhaps the creative response, of the objects themselves in order for the desired state of affairs to occur. An obvious instance of this is illness. If I am ill, I have some power over my body—inasmuch as my attitudes might help in the healing process and inasmuch as I might take curative measures—but the cells in my body also have lives of their own. They may or may not respond to my intentions to heal.

In fact, even a conscious decision to raise an arm, despite possible feelings to the contrary, is an act of invitational agency. When we consciously decide to raise our arms, the cells in our arms must cooperate, and for some of us they do not. Those with muscular dystrophy know this all too well, but even those without this disease know that, sometimes, simple bodily motions do not occur as we wish. At least with respect to conscious movements of our bodies, "unilateral agency" is actually invitational agency, the desired outcome of which has a high probability and likelihood of occurring. In deciding to raise our arms, we invite our arms to rise, and they usually do rise.

Still, for the sake of discussion, let us for the moment assume that unilateral agency does exist. If the world is God's body, and if God thus acts in the world, what kind of agency does God exercise: unilateral or invitational?

In relation to human life, many Christians will say that God's agency is invitational. We speak of God's agency as a call to love God and to love others as we love ourselves. We presuppose that we are free to respond or not respond to this call, that we may sin. By virtue of our freedom, we assume that in the short run divine purposes are actually divine hopes. We take it as our task to fulfill these hopes, to do the will of God "on earth as it is in heaven," presuming we could in fact do otherwise. If we are panentheists, we are *relational* panentheists.

With respect to the rest of nature, however, we can adopt a different perspective. With respect to subatomic particles, atoms, molecules, living cells, multicelled organisms, planets, stars, and black holes, we can assume that God's agency is unilateral rather than invitational. Here we will tend to believe that whatever happens in nature is a result of God's will. Despite the biblical notion that even nature is fallen, we will assume that evolution bears full witness to divine purposes. Here, if we are panentheists, we adopt an *emanationist* perspective.

I believe that the latter way of thinking is inappropriate. If we are to make sense of the fact that God in divine empathy "wishes things were otherwise," we must recognize that God's agency with respect to nonhuman nature, too, is and always has been invitational rather than unilateral. This is to suggest that a relational panentheism obtains even with regard to nonhuman nature. In order to develop this perspective further, it is helpful first to look at the way Arthur Peacocke construes divine agency and then turn to process theology.

Peacocke's Understanding of Divine Agency

Drawing from panentheism's mind-body analogy, Peacocke suggests that God acts in the world as a mind acts in and through its body. In using the analogy, he focuses on the agency that mental states have in expressing intentions and purposes through bodily activities (1984, 74–75; 1979, 133–138). Just as the meaning of a consciously initiated bodily action (raising an arm) must be determined by seeking the meaning or intention of the self that did the initiating, so the meaning of the "nexus of physical events which constitute the world" must be determined by seeking the intentions of God. Here, Peacocke seems to be adopting a modified emanationist perspective. He seems to be saying not that the body of God expresses the "stuff" of God but that indeed it infallibly expresses the intentions of God.

But qualifications are in order. Peacocke recognizes "that many individual events in our bodies, and many regular patterns of events, occur without any conscious control by the self" (1979, 137). He recognizes that, analogously, we see many events in nature that seem not to exemplify any specific purposes of God. Yet he implies that even these events are revelatory of general purposes of God. The mind-body analogy is still applicable, for it applies "both to those patterns of events in the world initiated by the purposes of God and to those many other individual events and some regular patterns of events which cannot be regarded as initiated by a specific purpose of God—even though they are what they are because God created them so" (1979, 138).

Does this mean that all nonhuman outcomes of evolutionary process—even if less revelatory of specific divine purposes than others—are nonetheless the product of divine unilateral agency? On this matter Peacocke's thought moves in two quite different directions. There are two strands to his thinking: one concerning immanence, which suggests to me a unilateral model, and the other concerning the role of chance and self-creativity in evolution, which opens the door for an invitational model.

In explaining divine immanence, Peacocke images God as "exploring" a gamut of possibilities for created existence much in the manner that a composer—J. S. Bach, for example—explores possibilities for a fugue. Just as Bach begins with an arrangement of notes for a very simple tune and then elaborates and expands that arrangement into a fugue by a variety of devices, so God begins with an arrangement of matter imbued with divinely donated potential and elaborates and expands that arrangement into an evolutionary process that produces, among other things, life on Earth and Homo sapiens within it. Peacocke stresses that creation is a continuous, open-ended process and that God is immanent within this process much as Bach is immanent within his fugue. He tells us that "God is in all the creative processes of his creation" and that "they are all equally 'acts of God.' " God is "everywhere and all the time present and active in them as their agent." The acts of nature are God's "acts" (1979, 204). They are acts of divine self-expression. Here Peacocke seems to speak as an emanationist panentheist who deems God's agency in nature unilateral.

In a different direction, however, Peacocke speaks of the role of "chance" in evolution, particularly biological, and in this respect his language opens the door for a relational model. Peacocke insists that biological evolution is open-ended and that in it "chance" plays an increasingly influential role. In this context "chance" refers to the unpredictable intersection of individual traits within a biological population (including those produced by mutations) and the factors in the environment in relation to which some of those traits will prove to be more adaptive than others. As chance plays a greater and greater role in biological evolution, God's own purposes are "at risk" (1984, 67). There was more chance, and hence more divine risk, in Pleistocene times than in Pennsylvanian times.

In speaking of this risk, Peacocke emphasizes the riskiness of allowing to come into existence free human beings who can clearly diverge from divine purposes or co-create in cooperation with God. But there are hints, at least as I read him, that the risk occurs even earlier in the evolutionary process. Peacocke notes that creativity plays a larger and larger role as evolution "becomes more and more focussed in the activity of the biological individual" (1984, 67). He tells us that there are "errors," "false trails," and "dead ends" in the evolutionary process (1984, 67). This suggests that from Peacocke's perspective there *may* be events that occur in the history of nature prior to human life that are *not* expressive of divine intentions. At least Peacocke opens the door to that line of thought.

Divine Agency in Process Theology

Process theologians pass through the door, and I think that we must as well. They believe that errors, dead ends, and false trails occur in the evolutionary process, not necessarily because God wills them, and not necessarily because God allows them, but rather because nature has creativity in its own right. Even with respect to nonhuman nature, process theologians are relational panentheists. They believe that the relation between God and the universe is—and has been from a beginningless past—an ongoing interaction between manifold creative agents: an all-caring, all-influential, and all-faithful agent, whom we name God, and countless other agents, including ourselves, who collectively form God's body. Because this option offers a way of showing how God is responsible but not indictable for the plight of the second pelican chick, we do well to explore it in more detail. I will proceed by looking at how process theologians understand biological evolution.

Process thinkers agree with Peacocke that the errors, false trails, and dead ends in evolution occur because of "chance." Moreover, they define chance as does Peacocke: as the unpredictable intersection of individual traits and environmental stresses (Birch 1987, 5). They then ask a further question: What property does nature possess such that unpredictable "accidents" can occur in the first place?

Their answer is creativity. In this context creativity means the act of actualizing possibilities, in ways not entirely predictable in advance, for integrating and thus responding to causal influences. An entity—a pulsation of energy in the depths of an electron, for example—is creative if, given a set of past circumstances by which it is about to be influenced, it can actualize one among two or more possibilities for synthesizing those influences. In fact this is the way physicist Henry Stapp suggests that subatomic matter works (Stapp 1977, 174; McDaniel 1983, 302–313). According to Stapp, quantum mechanics helps us to know in advance how a given energy pulsation will probably behave but not how it will actually behave until it thus behaves. Given the past circumstances, we must wait and see how the pulsation decides—albeit in an utterly nonconscious way—to respond. There seems to be an element of spontaneity, of creativity, even in the depths of matter. Process theologians propose that "chance" in biological evolution on Earth is rooted in creativity of this sort. While the general contours of evolution can be predicted as matters of statistical probability, the detailed course of evolution cannot be predicted or predetermined, even by God, because the agents of evolution—at least many of them, from subatomic events through living cells to multicelled organisms—have spontaneity in their own right.

Here the Christian might assent but then add that creativity in evolution is identical with God's creativity. This can be to adopt an emanationist perspective. It is also to run into problems of natural evil. To equate the creativity of nature—which obviously issues into much tragedy as well as much good—with the creativity of God is to call into question divine goodness. The best that one could say with this equation of worldly creativity with divine creativity is that the unfolding of the universe is divine play, the choreography of "a lonely cosmic dancer whose routine is all creatures and all worlds" (Smith 1958, 84). Could he reflect upon it, the second pelican chick would find little consolation in this perspective, nor would the Jewish boy hanging from the gallows at Auschwitz.

For purposes of theodicy, let us assume that worldly creativity and divine creativity are different. The task for process theologians, then, is to show how God is active in a creative evolutionary process whose creativity is different from God's own. In accomplishing this task, they agree with Peacocke that the creative activity of God is best conceived as continuous and ever present, that divine creativity has been at work from the beginning of our cosmic epoch, and that the presence of this creativity is responsible for the fact that there is a universe and a world as we know it. For them as for Peacocke, God did create the world.

Yet, for them, God did not create the world out of nothing. Rather he—or, better, she—created the world out of a chaos of energy events present at the beginning of our cosmic epoch (Peacocke 1979, 142). At that stage the chaos was within her as part of her body, and while it was devoid of order and novelty, it was nevertheless possessive of its own ability to actualize possibilities, its own creativity. By availing the chaos of possibilities for order and novelty, God gave birth to the universe within herself, and the birth process continues. In the words of Paul, even today creation "groans in all its parts as if in the pangs of childbirth. Not only so, but even we . . . are groaning inwardly" (Rom. 8:22–23, NEB).

For reasons that will be much clearer in the final chapter on postpatriarchal Christianity, I use the feminine pronoun purposefully, though I do not mean to imply that masculine language cannot also be helpful. Within contemporary Christian communities, different images can and should be used to indicate the all-loving God of Christian faith, female as well as male. As Sallie McFague shows, all these images are metaphorical (1987, 29–45). In dealing with the image of God as Creator, one reason for preferring female to male imagery can be stated here. As Peacocke rightly notes (1979, 142),

The concept of God as Creator has, in the past, been too much dominated by a stress on the externality of God's creative acts—he is regarded as creating something external to himself, just as a male fertilizes the womb from the outside. But mammalian females, at least, create within themselves and the growing embryo resides within the female body, and this is a proper corrective to the masculine picture— it is an analogy of God creating the world within herself.

Many process theologians agree with Peacocke's analysis. More than a few process theologians are women, and they, like Cobb and Griffin (1976, 135), find that an exclusive use of masculine imagery of God "distorts our images and represses women." Particularly with respect to a panentheistic image of God as Creator, it is helpful to imagine God as a divine Mother who creates the world within herself rather than a Father who creates it outside himself (see also McFague 1987, 97–123).

Of course, whether God be imaged as Father or Mother, a "creation out of chaos" perspective diverges from classical, postbiblical Christianity. Recognizing this fact, process theologians argue that such a perspective nevertheless warrants the designation "Christian" because, among other things, it is continuous with the earliest strands of biblical thinking concerning creation. As Birch points out, "where the technical term 'create' is used in the Bible, the issue of *creatio ex nihilo* is not raised" (1966, 89). The doctrine was first articulated in the intertestamental period and later elaborated by Irenaeus and Augustine in order to counter the idea that matter was the source of evil. Cobb and Griffin argue that creation out of chaos is more biblical, that it is suggested "by more Old Testament passages than those supporting the doctrine of creation out of nothing" (1976, 65). And on this Peacocke concurs. Despite the fact that he prefers the ex nihilo perspective because of its emphasis on the absolute dependence of the world on God, he notes a consensus among scholars that "the principal emphasis in ancient Israel's understanding of creation was that Yahweh created order, a cosmos, out of chaos" (1979, 82, 141).

If we assume that several different understandings of creation can coexist within contemporary Christianity and that, given its biblical precedents, a creation out of chaos model is one among them, I believe Christians can accept such a model. Then the question becomes: *How* does God create out of chaos? In what manner, unilaterally or by invitation?

Process theologians propose that God created the world, and continues to do so, by beckoning or invitation. Specifically, God is present in and through aims or purposes, felt in a conscious or nonconscious way by creatures themselves, to integrate other causal influences in ways that promote order where order is needed and novelty where it is needed. These aims or purposes are goals from

which creatures may diverge or by which they can be drawn, relative
to their own capacities for creative self-determination. As human life
attests, creatures may indeed choose aims other than those willed by
God. In any case, the creatures must themselves actualize the possibilities. God's creativity lies in offering the possibilities, which are the
means through which God exercises divine guidance in the world.
The divinely derived possibilities are not goals that violate a creature's creativity; rather, they are goals for a creature's creativity.
God creates by inviting creatures to integrate causal influences and
thus create themselves.

To better understand this perspective, the musical analogy offered
by Peacocke can be extended. If God is a composer or conductor,
God is, as Birch puts it, "writing a score a few bars ahead of the
orchestra, taking into account their harmonies and disharmonies as
he proposes the next movement of the music" (1987, 13). A score
consists of possibilities for playing music, and it may change as the
music changes, though always it is the best for the context. As
exercised through these possibilities, the power of God is the power
of persuasion to harmonize the whole and to inspire all musicians to
play their best, given their capacities. God needs the world in order
for the music to be played; the world needs God in order to have an
ongoing score that offers direction and novelty. At a given moment
in the history of nature, God does not perform the music ex nihilo;
rather, God performs it with the help of creatures whose very lives,
at an earlier stage, she called into existence out of chaos.

Clearly, the process perspective hinges on the assumption that
creatures can feel possibilities and have aims in the first place. It
hinges not only on a transcendence of mechanistic images of nature
but on a particular alternative to mechanism, one that emphasizes
the anticipatory dimension of individual creatures within natural
processes. Here "creatures" are finite seats of creative sentience.
They include individual energy events within the depths of atoms,
living cells within plants, and multicelled animals such as human
beings. None of these creatures should be understood atomistically;
all are what they are in relation to other creatures and God. All are
influenced—that is, caused—by other creatures, which are themselves influenced, or caused, by still others, ad infinitum. A creature's
creativity lies in integrating the influences from which it emerges,
sometimes in novel ways. God's aims for the creature are experienced by the creature as possibilities for integration. Hence God
works with the causality of the world, not against it or apart from
it. God is found in the anticipatory—or goal-directed dimension—of
creaturely existence.

In human life, this anticipatory dimension is most apparent. The possibilities that we derive from God are experienced as inwardly felt calls or promptings toward the fullness of life relative to the situation at hand, toward what the Bible calls shalom. It is as if within each of us there is a beckoning light—a still, small voice—that calls us beyond who we have been (and perhaps beyond who society tells us we ought to be) toward who we can be if we are true to ourselves and to God. Our awareness of this voice is provoked or inhibited by social circumstances and environmental contexts. For some, it is nurtured by the church and participation in sacraments; for others, it is obstructed by them. In any case, often we are called by the inner light to repent, to turn around, from past ways of being in order to better love God, the world, and ourselves. Of course, the words "light" and "voice" are metaphorical. They refer to an invisible attractant that lies within each of us: an inwardly felt lure toward self-actualization in community with other people, with the rest of nature, and with the divine spirit. This lure is God immanent in us as an agent of our well-being, as a Holy Spirit.

Because the very aim of this Holy Spirit is for creaturely well-being, and because Christians see a compassionate aim of this sort as decisively exemplified in Jesus, the inwardly felt Spirit can also be named "the Logos" or "the universal Christ" (Cobb 1975, 17–94). Indeed, in keeping with the broad connotations of the word "universal," process theologians suggest that this Spirit—the cosmic Christ—is also present in nonhuman life. The lure of God's Spirit is that by which nonhuman organisms are inspired to live from moment to moment with some degree of satisfaction relative to their situations. Through the immanence of this Spirit the second pelican chick is inspired to seek satisfaction, and through it the first chick— the competitor born two days earlier—is similarly inspired. In the struggle between the two chicks, God is on the side of each, desirous of the well-being of both. The Holy Spirit is the eros toward life by which biological (including sexual) eros is itself elicited, and to which it is responsive. As fully biological creatures, humans, too, experience God in this way: a way that has too often been neglected in dualistic versions of Christian self-understanding.

The lure of God is present within inorgánic matter. Here, of course, the credibility of those for whom inorganic matter is "lifeless" and "inert" is strained, for clearly something lifeless cannot in any way experience or respond to aims or purposes, divine or otherwise. But in its depths matter is not utterly inert, and contemporary physics, particularly quantum mechanics, invites us to infer that there is a kind of purposive activity even within allegedly lifeless matter (McDaniel 1983). The energy events that constitute matter are not simply products of their pasts; they are actualizations of

possible futures. In and through possibilities available for actualiza-
tion by matter in its depths, God is present within the depths of
matter.

For creatures at the inorganic level, however, the invitation to
create is for the most part irresistible. Energy pulsations within the
depths of matter have little ability to resist divine purposes; hence
much of what has happened in cosmic and chemical evolution may
be attributed to divine intentions. Here the music of creation may
indeed **be** like a fugue, the movements of which are beautiful and yet
predictable. Still, the creatures themselves must play the music,
which accounts for the slight unpredictability in inorganic processes.

With life on Earth, however, the role of the creaturely musicians
becomes even more pronounced. The fugue becomes an open-ended
symphony, and the divine composer-conductor becomes an improvi-
sor. The capacities for resistance, as well as co-creativity, increase,
and the divine purposes become much more like divine hopes. In
ways not evident before, what Christians have traditionally called a
"fall" becomes possible.

And here the plight of the second pelican chick becomes relevant.
Birch and Cobb propose that "the symbol of the fall . . . can properly
be used to describe particular occurrences in the evolutionary historical process" and that the coming of animal life was itself such an
occurrence (1981, 120). Prior to animal life, they say, there was little
if any suffering as we know it, and there was much greater stability.
"Animal life introduced greatly increased instability into an otherwise regular world." The evolution of animal life was a "fall" in that
it was "the occurrence of a new level of order and freedom bought
at the price of suffering." Yet it was an advance as well, because it
introduced greater opportunities for harmony and intensity of experience, greater opportunities for creativity and sentience. It was, so
Birch and Cobb say, a "fall upward" (1981, 120–121). The second
pelican chick suffers from this fall.

Here two questions emerge. Did the benefits of this fall upward
outweight the costs? And was the fall upward willed by God? Process
theologians answer yes to both questions. They see the lure of God
at work in the evolution of life on Earth, including animal life, and
they believe that the benefits of increased creativity and sentience for
animals were worth the costs to the rest of creation, to animals
themselves, and to God.

The costs to God—at least to a God who is all-loving—must have
been great. In the first place, the beckoning of the world into animal
life involved risk, a relinquishment of divine control. No doubt as
soon as animal life emerged—and much more dramatically with
vertebrate life—much began to occur in evolution that was difficult
if not impossible for God to harmonize. In particular, strategies for

survival emerged—such as that of the white pelicans—that could not easily be harmonized with God's desire for the well-being of each individual creature on its own terms. Like a mother who cares for all her children but whose children must fight one another for a single piece of bread, God found herself—and undoubtedly still finds herself—on the side of individual creatures whose own interests were, and are, mutually exclusive.

In the second place, the luring of the world into animal life involved an increase in divine suffering. If one considers the countless billions of painful experiences suffered by creatures since animal life began, and imagine in each instance that suffering was shared by an all-empathic God, the suffering of God staggers the imagination.

Why, then, did God not lure creation into forms of pain-free animal life? The answer, according to Cobb and Griffin, is that God could not do so. Built into the very nature of life are necessary correlations among its following five dimensions: (1) the capacity for self-determination; (2) the capacity for intrinsic good, which is the enjoyment of harmony and intensity; (3) the capacity for intrinsic evil, which among other things is the suffering of unwanted pain; (4) the capacity for instrumental evil, which includes harming others; and (5) the capacity for instrumental good, which includes aiding others. If any of these given capacities increases, the others increase proportionately; "the good cannot be had without the bad" (1981, 73). These correlations are necessary rather than contingent, which means they are not dependent on choice, even divine choice. Given that God lured creation into animal life, God had to take the risk that with the increased capacities for sentience enjoyed by animal life, there would be increased possibilities for pain. There was no option: either advanced animal life with pain or no animal life at all.

For those who have enjoyed at least a modicum of richness of experience, the divine risk seems to have been worth it. Between suffering and joy, on the one hand, and nonexistence on the other, we are glad we have had suffering and joy. But are there not some for whom joy has not outweighed suffering, and for whom nonexistence may be a preferable option? Was the risk worth it for them? Was it worth it for the second pelican chick? It was worth it, I believe, only if there is redemption.

IV. The Redemption of Pelicans

Just as God's love for nature cannot be limited to the whole of nature at the expense of nature's parts, so God's redemption of nature cannot be so limited. If the love of God is anything like that of an all-loving parent, God would want to redeem the parts as well as the whole. As the Mother of all pelicans, she would want to redeem the individual backup chick as well as the entire family of pelicans.

But whole-part language is itself misleading. While nature is a complex network of interdependent creatures, it is not a "whole" in the sense of being a "completed" or a "perfectly harmonious" assemblage of parts. Nature is an unfinished evolutionary process and therefore incomplete. And at least from the perspective of sentient prey in predator-prey relations, it is a disharmonious process, a broken process in which the good of one is evil for another. When we speak of God's redemption of nature, let us have in mind those animate "parts of the whole" whose lives on their own terms were broken because most of their felt needs were unfulfilled. The second pelican chick can be our paradigm.

The word "redemption" has different meanings. It can mean (1) freedom from the consequences of sin, in which case it applies almost exclusively to humans. But it can also mean (2) freedom from what distresses or harms, (3) contribution to lives beyond one's own, and (4) transformation into an improved state of existence. We do well to consider whether redemption in these additional instances can apply to the pelican chick.

First, consider redemption in the sense of freedom from what distresses or harms. Clearly the backup chick can be redeemed in this sense, and apparently without the help of God. For death itself provides him with freedom from the suffering he underwent in his brief existence on Earth. Death can be a friend, a redemptive end to his brief misery. Still, if this is the only sense in which the pelican chick is redeemed, it is not clear that the risk taken by God in luring the world into animal life was worth it *for the chick.* Given the improbability of his surviving with satisfaction, it is possible that it would have been better *for him* if he had never existed in the first place, so as not to have undergone the pain that required a redemptive death. The question is whether the intensity of life in pain is worth it for a creature, even if that life is devoid of harmony. In concluding paragraphs, I will return to this question. For the moment, however, it is advisable to reflect upon redemption in the other two senses.

Redemption as Contribution to Lives Beyond One's Own

Consider redemption as contribution to value beyond oneself: in this case, contribution to the lives of other creatures. In being part of an evolutionary process in which white pelicans have survived for thirty million years, the backup chick serves succeeding generations of pelicans. Without backup chicks such as he, there would be no insurance policy for the survival of pelicans as a species. Moreover, he serves the interests of parasites who reside within his body before and after death and of creatures who feed on him. Upon death his bodily chemicals are absorbed into the Earth, and they then nourish other creatures. He lives on, not as a subject for himself, but as a dispersal of energy for others. He is an "innocent sacrificed to preserve a line, a blood sacrifice perishing that others might live" (Rolston 1987, 144). We might say that his life is "redeemed" inasmuch as he acquires this instrumental value for myriad other creatures, "redeemed" as a contributor to an evolutionary ecosystem much greater than he.

But there is a problem with this line of thought. The acquisition of instrumental value for other living beings—important as it is— does not necessarily make the experiment of life worth it for the chick. After all, he feels that he is an end in himself, not simply a means to other ends. His life may serve others, but he seems to gain no pleasure from this fact, or even to be cognizant of it. He simply struggles to survive, as if his survival mattered in its own right. While we might find the chick's instrumental value quite meaningful, this meaning is not redemption for the chick on his terms. The aims to survive, felt by the chick himself, are frustrated rather than served by the evolutionary ecosystem of which he is a part. If we speak of his redemption as service to the ecosystem and to his own species, we neglect his own interests and needs as an individual struggling to survive for his own sake.

There is still another way, however, in which the chick might contribute to a value beyond himself, a way that does not involve neglect of his own interests and needs. The chick can contribute to the life of God. I have already suggested that as each living being takes into account its environment moment by moment, living out its aims and needs, its experiences are shared by God. This occurs in the receptive side of God, that side which is limitlessly empathic. As we think about this receptive side, process theologians propose a further image, one that taps into some of our deepest hopes for communal wholeness. They suggest that as each and every creature is empathetically felt by God, the creature's momentary experiences are appreciated and harmonized, as much as is possible, with the felt needs and experiences of every other creature. Thus, the receptive dimension of God is an ultimate, ongoing intense harmony. The quality of this harmony is affected by what it receives, and it includes tragedy. It is best characterized by the word "beauty": the adventure of the universe as One (Whitehead 1933, 380).

Perhaps as contributing to God, then, the pelican chick might find redemption. For as divine harmonizing occurs, the chick's experiences are linked with everything else in the universe in a way that transcends the brokenness of creation as he experienced it. A harmony is achieved in God that is not achieved on Earth. This eschato-logical harmonization does not involve a forgetfulness of the chick's life on its own terms. Rather, to whatever extent possible, it involves a creative integration of his life on *his* terms with all other lives on *their* terms. It is the realization in divine experience of an eschatolog-ical community of love. The chick is redeemed by contributing to, and being remembered in, the everlasting life of God.

It is important to recognize that this additional type of contribu-tive redemption does, indeed, involve divine power: the power to bear suffering and to creatively integrate worldly experiences into divine beauty. The very Mother who was limited in her ability to create life without discord is powerful enough to redeem lives of discord, at least as subjects in her own experience. This kind of "power" transcends the image of unilateral control. It is a power to receive and then create something new. Here God does actualize possibilities of her own, God becomes not only a composer and conductor but a musician in her own right. Hers is the power not to prevent the crosses her children must suffer but to actualize an ever-dynamic resurrection within her own experience: a resurrection in which each child is loved and appreciated for his or her own sake. Here the image of an all-loving Parent is appropriate, whether that parent is imaged as Mother or Father. In what follows I will continue to use female imagery for God, both for consistency and as a much-needed corrective of, and supplement to, the preponderance of male imagery in the Christian heritage.

But is this redemption sufficient to make the risk of life worth it for the chick? After all, the chick himself does not experience the resurrection, at least as a subject for himself. His life may be re-deemed in the sense that it contributes to the adventure of the universe as One, but he does not experience this as a fulfillment of his own felt needs. As an individual seat of awareness with needs of his own, he simply dies. Is there any way to imagine the pelican as experiencing his own redemption? Must he experience his redemp-tion if his life is to have meaning?

Asking these questions, let us consider the possibility that the pelican partakes of some sort of renewal after death in which he is allowed to fulfill those needs for survival and satisfaction that were so brutally frustrated in his earthly life. Here we consider the fourth meaning of redemption: transformation into a new state of affairs.

Transformation Into a New State of Affairs

This kind of redemption, too, would involve the power of God, for the transformation occurs through the gift of new and often unan-ticipated possibilities for wholeness amid brokenness. In this life,

many of us already know "redemption" in this sense. We find ourselves in situations of hopelessness and, like slaves in Egypt, we
discover new possibilities for hope amid our hopelessness, new possibilities for a promised land. Process theologians would say that such
refreshment in this life is in fact a gift from God, the result of divine
grace. For the lure of God is an ever-present storehouse of new
possibilities. This view is consistent with, and indebted to, much of
the prophetic biblical tradition, which also sees God as the source
of new and unanticipated possibilities (Brueggemann 1978). Indeed,
as Ugaritic scholar Loren Fisher has argued, redemption as the gift
of new possibilities for order out of chaos is inseparable from what
the Bible usually means by creation. If by "creation" we mean creation out of chaos, "creation . . . is redemption" (quoted in Peacocke
1979, 82).

It follows that if divine creation is to some extent dependent on
creaturely response, so is divine redemption. Increasingly, as creatures have evolved who are free to diverge from divine aims, they
must themselves respond to the divine lure toward redemption, if in
fact they are to be redeemed. A doctrine of co-creativity needs to be
complemented by one of co-redemptivity. In order to be redeemed,
we must ourselves respond to divine grace—and perhaps other creatures must too.

But, of course, this may be a moot point for the pelican chick. No
doubt he might like the opportunity to respond to redemptive possibilities offered by God, but he must have some context for doing so.
If he is to enjoy redemption, he must live in some way beyond his
own earthly death so as to be given further opportunities to co-create
with God.

While historically more Christians than not have hoped for
renewal after death, whether in the form of a heavenly joy or resurrection of the dead, more often than not this renewal has been
conceived as a gift to be enjoyed only by human beings. A contemporary theology of nature that shares in this hope cannot be satisfied
with such anthropocentrism. Just as we hope that other human
beings, given their propensities and needs, find appropriate fulfillment in life beyond death, we must hope that kindred creatures,
given their propensities and needs, find fulfillment in life after death
too.

Let us be clear about this hope. The hope is not that all creatures
share in the same kind of fulfillment beyond death. Rather it is that
all creatures share in that kind of fulfillment appropriate to their own
interests and needs. What a pelican chick might know as a fulfillment
of needs would have its own kind of harmony and intensity, one quite
different from what we humans might know. If there is a pelican
heaven, it is a *pelican* heaven. And the hope is not necessarily that

all living beings live forever as subjects in their own right; rather, it is that they live until they enjoy a fulfillment of their needs as creatures. Neither pelicans nor humans need live forever. What spawns the hope for life after death is not a desire for immortality but rather a recognition that so many lives—indeed, the vast majority—end in incompleteness. Given the inescapable lure to live with wholeness and satisfaction, a lure that itself is the immanence of a creative God, one life does not seem to be enough.

In recent times, of course, it has not been fashionable for Protestant Christian theologians, much less those interested in a theology of nature, to speculate on the possibility of life after death. One exception to this generalization, however, is John Cobb. More than twenty years ago Cobb developed a process-oriented Christian natural theology in which, among other things, he tried to show the possibility of life after death using the philosophical conceptuality of Whitehead (1965, 63–70). In so doing, he drew upon Whitehead's distinction between the animal psyche and the animal brain, plus Whitehead's recognition that there could be relations among actualities not mediated by bodies in three-dimensional space. Cobb's intention was not to show that psychic existence is necessarily renewed after death but that reality may well be constituted in a way that allows for such renewal. He agreed with Whitehead that the question of whether or not there *is* renewal must be decided on empirical evidence.

There is no need to rehearse Cobb's argument in this chapter. It is important to note, however, that in developing his view Cobb acknowledged Whitehead's own suspicion of the view that for all humans there is a renewal of personal existence after death and for all other animals there is no such renewal. In Cobb's words, "Whitehead is doubtful that so sharp a line can be drawn between animals and humans that there is real warrant for affirming total extinction of all animals and survival of all humans" (1965, 64). The implication, I believe, is that Cobb is doubtful as well. If human psyches survive death in any way, there is little reason to think that nonhuman animal psyches do not.

Few if any process theologians have developed the implications for nonhuman animals of the possibility of life after death. For that matter, many process theologians are skeptical that there is any life after death at all, despite its possibility. They follow Hartshorne in seeing redemption as contribution to the life of God. Nevertheless, it seems to me that the question of whether or not animal psyches survive death is relevant to the question of whether or not the pelican chick can enjoy his own redemption. The question is relevant to a theology of nature.

If the chick does continue in some way, and if God is immanent within him as a lure toward fulfillment in that state just as God was immanent before, it becomes imaginable that, in time, the pelican would experience his own fulfillment of needs and interests, his own redemption. The risk taken by God in luring the world into life, which set the stage for pelican life, was then worth it, even for this chick. Without the fall upward into animal life by which he himself was victimized, there would have been no eschatological fulfillment, for him or for us.

Whether or not we choose to hope for life after death depends on what we take to be evidence. Some turn to parapsychology, and this may be a promising avenue to explore (Heaney 1984). In any case Christians can also turn to accounts concerning the resurrection of Jesus as one resource on which to rest their hopes that, in fact, the possibility of life after death is an actuality. Still, the hope remains a hope. It is not necessarily a hope for everlasting existence of a living being, a prospect that many humans understandably find quite undesirable. There is indeed a need within the life process itself for death, for cessation, for an end to the journey. Rather, the hope is for a continuation of a sentient being's journey until completeness, shalom, is realized, after which death can be welcomed. If hope of this sort does not subvert our zest for life on Earth, it is a hope by which we might live as we encounter nature "groaning in travail." It is not a fact concerning which we can or need claim certainty.

V. The Fulfillment of Life's Eros

This chapter began with the pelican chick and has returned to him again and again. We do well to end with him. Rolston writes that "the luckless backup chick suffers and dies, a minor pelican tragedy, but this sort of thing, amplified over and over, makes nature seem cruel and ungodly" (1987, 140). Struck by the truth of Rolston's claim, I have argued that God suffers with the backup chick and with all sentient creatures, and that, while God is responsible for the fact that the chick exists in the first place, God may not be indictable for the chick's fate, at least if the chick is redeemed. In the final part of the previous section, I suggested two ways of understanding redemption that rely on divine power: (1) redemption as contribution to the divine life, which relies on God's power to creatively synthesize creaturely experiences, and (2) redemption as the chick's own renewal after death, which relies on God's power to lure him into a wholeness beyond the brokenness he experienced in life. The latter possibility is a form of redemption for which I hope, but on which I do not want to rest the meaning of redemption. Rather, I rest it

on the first meaning. I conclude by noting two reasons leading me
to hope that, even if there is not a renewal after death, the backup
chick's life is nevertheless worthwhile, even on his own terms.

The first has to do with what we—and, I suggest, other living
beings as well—find meaningful and hence worthwhile in life. It is
richness of experience, which itself consists of intensity as well as
harmony. In human life at least, to partake of intensity as well as
harmony, and thus to enjoy richness of experience, is not simply to
risk suffering; it is also to *know* certain kinds of suffering, both
psychological and physical. There is something rich, though not
pleasurable, in grief born of empathy and in sweat born of physical
labor.

I do not in the least want to suggest that all suffering enhances
richness. Much suffering—particularly that which is intense and
which is undergone involuntarily—does not contribute to an individual's well-being at all. All things considered, things would have been
better—for the individual, for us if we are sensitive, and for an
all-loving God—if circumstances had been otherwise. But the very
fact that some suffering does contribute to what we know as richness
of experience suggests that we should be very cautious in evaluating
the interests of other humans and nonhuman creatures. We should
let them speak for themselves. Because our nonhuman friends cannot
speak in languages we understand, we should be wary of concluding
that things would have been better had they never existed at all, and
thus that, if their lives are to have any meaning at all, they must
survive death in order to find satisfaction. Even if there is no renewal
after death, their lives—and ours as well—may have enough richness
of experience in the form of intensity to make them worth living,
even if that richness could be much improved by an addition of
harmony.

The second reason why it is not necessary that life be renewed after
death in order for life to be worth living pertains to the ultimate
meaning of life. It is bold and presumptuous to speak of life's "ultimate" meaning, but I will attempt to do so anyway. I believe that
the ultimate meaning of life lies not in a fulfillment of our individual
needs, important as that fulfillment is (not only to us but to God),
but rather in our contribution to the divine life. It is not that God
is a monarch whose vanity we must serve or that God is a patriarch
in whose service we are mere vassals. Rather, it is that God is a living,
ecological Whole in whom our own longings for wholeness—and the
longings of other creatures as well—are fulfilled. In the model I have
been developing in this chapter, God is not simply the mind of the
universe, God is the heart of the universe, and we along with other
creatures are the body of this heart. According to the *Oxford English
Dictionary,* heart means mind in the widest sense, including capaci-

ties for feeling and volition as well as thought (1970, 159). In a sense that resembles this understanding of heart, the Bible speaks of "the heart of God" twenty-six times (*Harper's Bible Dictionary* 1985, 377). As we use the mind-body analogy to understand the relation between God and the world, this biblical metaphor can help us today to overcome some of the sterile connotations of the word "mind" in its narrower senses. At a deep level, we can recognize that our own hearts—and perhaps that of the pelican chick as well—long for union with the divine Heart. We can understand the very eros of life as a desire to be part of that harmony and intensity—that vital, partly tragic, all-compassionate, cosmic beauty—that is God's life. In traditional language, we long to contribute "to the glory of God."

The God who is thus glorified need not be imagined as above or beyond the universe, though in a contemporary context there can and should be a variety of images, some traditional and some not. God can equally or alternatively be imagined as the heart of the universe, that is, at its center or core. She may be considered "large," not because she has the power of a unilateral king but because she is on the side of nature and of life. Her largeness is her largesse, her large-heartedness, her luring power, her grace. This largesse is expressed in her power to creatively transform, as best she can, the chaos of that into which life has evolved into a wholeness that fulfills life's yearnings.

It seems to me that the value of our lives must finally lie in the fulfillment of our own yearnings for harmony and intensity—and the fulfillment of the yearnings of other creatures as well—in a larger context, in the heart of the universe. Of this fulfillment, too, we can be trustful but not certain. The very model of God developed in this chapter is the product of hope or trust, not certainty. For when it comes to thinking about God, "we see in a mirror dimly" (1 Cor. 13:12). The most cursory survey of the manifold images of God that have appeared in the various world religions suggests that God is a multifaceted mystery. Within Christian communities, attempts to conceive God are tentative attempts to "model a mystery" and thus love God with our minds. Amid our explorations, we need to be cognizant of the fact that our minds are quite limited, that most of what we say is metaphorical, that much if not all of what we say may miss the mark completely, and that in all probability there is much more to the mystery than we comprehend. Nevertheless, as Christians who dare to believe that the divine Heart is Jesus-like, we can rightly hope that the divine mystery, whatever its other aspects, is all-loving and, for pelicans as well as humans, all-redemptive.

2

A Life-centered Ethic

Of the five to ten million species that share our planet, the Earth is likely to lose "at least one quarter, possibly one third, and conceivably one half" within the foreseeable future of the next century or so. This loss "will represent the biggest setback to the planetary complement of species since the first flickerings of life almost four billion years ago," and it will be caused, not by climatic quirks or other natural forces, but rather by a single species, *Homo sapiens.* So writes Norman Myers (1986, 101), a consultant to the World Council of Churches and well-known conservation biologist.

The somber implications of this warning are only slightly reduced by the fact that some members of the accused species, including Myers himself, are working against almost insurmountable odds to reverse the trend. In association with organizations such as the World Wildlife Fund and the International Union for the Conservation of Nature and Natural Resources, preservationists spend their time and money working to protect the habitats, and hence the future, of threatened and endangered creatures around the world. These include—to list mammals alone—the chimpanzee, African elephant, Asian elephant, Bactrian camel, Saudi Arabian gazelle, gorilla, howler monkey, giant panda, tiger, gray whale, wild yak, and mountain zebra.

Why work to save these creatures? Among other reasons, because such efforts are in human beings' self-interest. Through their germ plasm and genetic constituents, species of animals and plants represent a unique stock of natural resources: a stock from which—in the interests of medicine, agriculture, and industry—human beings may need to draw in the future, just as they have already so often drawn in the past. Myers tells us that each time we enter the neighborhood pharmacy, there is "roughly one chance in two that the medicine or pharmaceutical we purchase owes its origin, in one way or another, to wild species" (1986, 106).

But self-interest is not the only reason why at least some wildlife biologists spend their time and energy on wildlife preservation. Nor is it the reason why most of their cohorts in the animal welfare movement work to protect individual animals under human domestication—in science laboratories or factory farms, for example—from unnecessary pain or loss of life. Both groups recognize that, in addition to their instrumental value to us, animals have value in their own right. Many advocates of animal well-being are guided by a recognition that all life, not just human life, has intrinsic value.

Such activists exemplify what Charles Birch calls a "life-centered ethic" or, as I will also speak of it, a biocentric ethic. A life-centered ethic is rooted in respect for the intrinsic value of living beings: the value that each and every being has in and for itself. As practiced by Christians, this ethic will be accompanied by belief in a life-centered God, a God who, too, appreciates living beings in their intrinsic value. In a Christian context, the aim of a life-centered ethic is to revere life as deeply and richly, given our finitude, as does God in God's own limitless way. While any application of this ethic in practice must involve the recognition of a gradation of intrinsic value and a balancing of considerations of intrinsic value with those concerning instrumental value, practitioners of the ethic will begin with a recognition that *all* living things have value in their own right.

While some Christians might prefer that a postanthropocentric Christian ethic be called "theocentric" rather than "biocentric," I choose the latter term, not to deny the importance of God, but rather to emphasize that the God in whom Christians believe is on the side of life and ultimately concerned with the well-being of life. In chapter 1 I proposed that God is biocentric, interested in the well-being and redemption of pelicans as well as humans. Commitment to God is inseparable from a commitment to life. This means that Christians are centered in God, and hence "theocentric," to the extent that we center our lives around the aims and concerns of God, which are to promote the well-being of life. As I show in chapter 3, a spirituality that complements a life-centered ethic will not focus on God at the expense of the world. Rather, it will focus on the world as loved by God. It will be, to use the phrase of Matthew Fox and others, "creation-centered" (1983, 9–29).

Open as it must be to all life and, indeed, to the whole of creation, a Christian commitment to life need in no way exclude a special concern for human life. In a Christian context, any concern for the integrity of creation must include an unmitigated concern for justice among and peace between humans. It is no accident that the representatives at the General Assembly of the World Council of Churches at Vancouver in 1983 highlighted three values for contemporary Christian emphasis: peace, justice, and the integrity of creation. The World Council understandably emphasized that any theology of creation that ultimately excludes attention to peace and justice is shortsighted and unchristian.

Nevertheless, given the anthropocentric nature of so much of the Christian heritage, it is not uncommon to find Christian thinkers emphasizing peace and justice without attention to the integrity of creation. Much of Christian ethics has been practiced without attention to the integrity, or intrinsic value, of *nonhuman* creatures. Contemporary liberation theologies are an example. More often than not, they emphasize the liberation of human beings from oppression by other human beings, but they do not attend to the liberation of other living beings from human exploitation. Given the exigencies in which so much liberation theology emerges, this exclusion is understandable. But it is not necessary. The World Council's threefold schema rightly suggests that a liberation of human life can be complemented by a liberation of all life. In order to move toward a more inclusive liberation, it is important that sustained attention be given to what it can mean to respect nonhuman forms of life and to understand God in light of that respect. The purpose of this work is to provide that attention. The aim of this chapter is to develop the conceptual underpinnings of a life-centered ethic.

My intentions in undertaking this task are not simply to add to the stockpile of ethical problems with which Christians must deal. Nor are they to disperse our already limited moral energies. Instead, they are to make clear a new moral outlook—an "overall moral stance" to use the phrase of Gabriel Moran (1987, 697)—in which concerns for human life are understood in the broader context of concerns for life itself and in which trade-offs between the good of humans and the good of our nonhuman neighbors are minimized. With this outlook, Christians can better serve that liberation of life for which, in solidarity with other religions, we appropriately yearn.

The chapter is divided into four sections. The first reviews two movements in contemporary philosophy from which Christians can learn as we seek to develop postanthropocentric ethics. The remaining three attempt to articulate key ideas for a Christian biocentric ethic by asking, and attempting to answer, three questions: What characteristics must an organism possess in order to have intrinsic value? What is involved in a biocentric ethic that attempts to respect that value? And, given the necessity of violating the interests of nonhuman creatures, how can degrees of intrinsic value be distinguished?

I. Land Ethics and Animal Rights

There are numerous resources from which Christians can draw as we seek to envision and embody a biocentric ethic. We can turn to neglected traditions within Judaism, Christianity, and Islam, both biblical and postbiblical, highlighting the motif of stewardship; we can turn to feminism and other world religions; and we can turn to contemporary developments in art and science (Joranson 1984). In addition, we can learn from a contemporary movement in philosophy called "environmental philosophy," which has a growing number of advocates in Western Europe, the United States, and Australia. In particular, Christians interested in biocentric ethics can benefit from reviewing two developments in environmental philosophy: the "land ethics" movement and the "animal rights" tradition.

Land Ethics

Chief among the forerunners of environmental ethics in a Western philosophical setting is Aldo Leopold (1887–1948), forest and game manager for the U.S. Forest Service and later professor of game management at the University of Wisconsin. In his well-known *A Sand County Almanac,* Leopold argued that ethics should move beyond anthropocentrism toward a land ethic. He was among the first to coin the phrase "land ethic," and to this day his understanding of the phrase's content serves as a resource for environmental philosophers.[1]

Leopold believes that ethical codes and attitudes can and should evolve. What in one generation may seem unworthy of moral consideration can in the next generation seem worthy, and rightly so. Consider, for example, our attitude toward Greek ethics as the latter are illustrated in the *Odyssey.* "When god-like Odysseus returned from the wars of Troy," Leopold reminds us, "he hanged all on one rope a dozen slave girls." For Odysseus the hanging "involved no question of propriety." After all, the girls were suspected of misbehavior, and something had to be done to prevent future occurrences. But such behavior on Odysseus' part should not lead us to think that ancient Greece was without concepts of right and wrong. It was just that from Odysseus' perspective, as from that of any aristocratic Greek, relationships with slaves were not matters involving ethics. "The girls were property," and "the disposal of property was then, as now, a matter of expedience, not right and wrong" (Leopold 1949, 201).

In modern times many readers of this chapter would judge Odysseus' actions to be reprehensible. We realize that those who have been called "slaves" are human beings with integrity in their own right and that they have rights of their own, including the right not to be enslaved. We know, of course, that this realization is still not universally shared and that more subtle forms of enslavement still exist even in societies, including our own, where blatant slavery is condemned. Nonetheless, our own disdain for Odysseus' actions illustrates what Leopold would call an evolution in ethics, at least in principle. Our care, or at least our understanding of the appropriate scope and implications of care, has become more inclusive than it was in ancient Greece. According to Leopold, ethical progress occurs when beings once regarded in merely utilitarian terms—that is, as property—come to be regarded as appropriate subjects of moral regard, and codes of conduct follow. As Leopold puts it in discussing the transition from Greek society to our own, "During the three thousand years which have since elapsed, ethical criteria have been extended to many fields of conduct, with corresponding shrinkages in those judged by expediency only" (1949, 201).

Leopold's argument in proposing a land ethic is that it is time to expand even further our horizons of ethical regard. Our circle of concern must extend beyond the human sphere to the biosphere, cognizant of the fact that we are part of a "biotic community." The problem, Leopold writes, is that "there is as yet no ethic dealing with [humanity's] relation to land and to animals and plants which grow upon it. Land, like Odysseus' slave-girls, is still property. The land relation is still strictly economic, entailing privileges but not obligations" (1949, 201). Leopold's aim is to remedy this situation.

His proposed "land ethic" is decidedly communitarian or systemic in emphasis. As we extend our horizons of concern, Leopold suggests, our actions can be guided by the following principle: "A thing is right when it tends to preserve the integrity, stability, and beauty of the biotic community. It is wrong when it tends otherwise" (1949, 224–225). As is observed by J. Baird Callicott, a contemporary environmental philosopher and defender of Leopold, what is noteworthy about this principle "is that the good of the biotic *community* is the ultimate measure of the moral value, the rightness or wrongness, of actions" (1980, 381).

Leopold's emphasis on community has concrete implications for action. His principle suggests, for example, that it might be acceptable to hunt and kill white-tailed deer in order to protect a local ecosystem from the disintegrating effects of excessive population growth. And yet the principle also implies that it would be obligatory to protect individual members of an endangered species from extermination, since they are part of the integrity, stability, and beauty of a biotic community. In Callicott's words, "In every case the effect upon ecological *systems* is the decisive factor in the determination of the ethical quality of actions" (1980, 381).

With Leopold's interest in expanding ethical horizons beyond the human arena, of course, the ecologically oriented Christian will be naturally sympathetic. Indeed, a biocentric ethic involves precisely such expansion. And yet two questions naturally emerge from an encounter with Leopold. The first concerns value in nature. In what sense, after all, is the land valuable apart from its usefulness to human ends? The second concerns the status of the individual non-human organism. Given the emphasis on ecosystems or biotic communities that is so central to the land ethic, what is the moral status of the individual organism? Let us deal with the first question at this point and then turn to the second.

An environmental philosopher who has thought much about the issue of value in nature is Holmes Rolston III, whose concern with the plight of pelican chicks was my point of departure for developing a panentheist understanding of God in the first chapter. In numerous essays and also in his magnum opus *Environmental Ethics* (1988), Rolston laments that many influenced by the mechanistic worldview of industrial civilizations think of nonhuman nature as something devoid of value until assigned importance by human beings. The common but problematic assumption is that humans are the only creatures within creation with inherent value: "loci of value lost in a worthless environment" (1982, 151). Yet, though a Christian himself, Rolston does not counter this denial of nature's value, as might some Christians, by proposing that nature has worth because assigned it by God. Rather, he suggests that nature has value in itself, God or no God. He proposes that if we analyze our own experience of nature carefully, we will see that in many instances we experience nature, not merely as a recipient of value assignments, but as a "carrier of values" (1981, 113). If we are phenomenologically honest, we realize that nature carries values that supersede our own invention.

Rolston realizes that nature does not disclose its values to us apart from our subjective interpretations of it. With Kant and most philosophers since Kant, Rolston argues that our experience of nature is inevitably interpretive. Yet Rolston does suggest that, amid our interpretations, there is a receptive component. We do not simply create the nonhuman realities—plants, animals, and inorganic materials—that we interpret; rather, we experience these realities as given to us for interpretation, and in their givenness values are disclosed. Some of these values are aesthetic: "the mist that floats about an alpine cliff, spitting out lacy snowflakes, tiny exquisite crystals" (1981, 120). Some have to do with the unity and diversity of life and material forms: the "macroscopic web" of diverse life-forms that is matched by the unity revealed by the electron microscope or the X-ray spectrometer. And some pertain to the value living beings have in and for themselves: like that of the "tarantula at the Grand Canyon in 1896" whom the American naturalist and conservationist John Muir refused to kill (1981, 121). If we attend to and reflect upon our own experience and knowledge of nature, we see that "values are actualized in human relationships with nature, sometimes by [human] constructive activity depending on a natural support, sometimes by a sensitive, if an interpretive, appreciation of the characteristics of natural objects" (1981, 121).

Rolston is representative of most environmental ethicists in encouraging us to recognize the inherent worth of nature. Yet he, like Leopold and his advocates, warns against understanding it in atomistic or excessively individualistic terms. When people argue for the "intrinsic value" of a natural entity—that is, the value a natural entity might have for what it is in itself—Rolston is troubled. From his perspective "the 'for what it is in itself' facet of intrinsic value becomes problematic in a holistic web." It is "too internal and elementary; it forgets relatedness and externality." It neglects the fact that everything is good "in a role, in a whole" (1981, 128). Rolston's point is that individual mountains, plants, and animals do indeed have value apart from their usefulness to humans, but not in isolation from their environments. Their own intrinsic value is inseparable from their being organic parts of biotic communities and, ultimately, of nature as a whole.

Given this emphasis on nature as a whole, the second question mentioned above emerges: What, if anything, is the ethical status of *individual* nonhuman organisms, as they exist in and for themselves?

Animal Rights

Some proponents of the land ethic—Callicott, for example—are suspicious of ethical preoccupations with individual nonhuman creatures. They see it as symptomatic of a Western individualistic bias. Callicott does not deny that individual creatures can have a place as individuals in the sphere of ethical regard. But he says that when we are concerned with them, it is not their well-being as individuals that should be our concern. Rather, it is the well-being of the biotic community of which they are a part and to which they contribute. Taking Leopold's land ethic as paradigmatic for environmental ethics as such, Callicott insists that "environmental ethics locates ultimate value in the 'biotic community' and assigns differential moral value to the constitutive individuals relative to that standard" (1980, 337; cf. Callicott 1988).

Here we cannot settle the question of what rightly or wrongly belongs within the purview of environmental ethics understood as a subdiscipline within philosophy. But we can highlight those traditions in philosophy that point toward a postanthropocentric ethic, and in this context it is important to recognize that there exists a tradition that *is* interested in the interests of individual creatures, in particular animals under human dominion. Though not all its advocates prefer the language of "rights" in proposing that we recognize our obligations to animals, many do. For that reason we can call it the "animal rights" movement or, alternatively, the "animal liberation" movement, borrowing a phrase from Peter Singer (1975).

If Aldo Leopold is the mentor of the land ethic tradition, so Albert Schweitzer (1875–1965) could be that of the animal rights movement (Blackstone 1980, 304). Perhaps one reason Schweitzer has not played this role is that, in point of fact, the rights of animals have been defended by minority traditions in philosophy at least since the eighteenth century. Nevertheless, in advancing his reverence-for-life ethic in the early part of our century, Schweitzer well anticipates the concerns of contemporary animal rights advocates. Schweitzer writes:

> When abuse of animals is widespread, when the bellowing of thirsty animals in cattle cars is heard and ignored, when cruelty still prevails in many slaughterhouses, when animals are clumsily and painfully butchered in our kitchens, when brutish people inflict unimaginable torments upon animals and when some animals are exposed to the cruel games of children, all of us share in the guilt (quoted in Blackstone 1980, 306).

Schweitzer's interest in eliminating the unnecessary suffering of individual animals is at the heart of the animal rights movement.

Peter Singer is among the movement's most articulate spokespersons. His well-known *Animal Liberation: A New Ethics for Our Treatment of Animals* (1975) deals specifically with the suffering inflicted on individual animals in scientific experimentation, agribusiness, and industry. The examples he gives—ranging from pain experiments on rhesus monkeys and dogs, through the inhumane conditions in which pigs and cattle are reared for food consumption, to the blinding of rabbits in the testing of cosmetics—are staggering both in terms of the pains suffered by the animals and in terms of the numbers of animals affected. He argues that there is no reason in principle why the suffering of our kindred creatures should matter less than our own. The fact that some animals cannot reason or talk in language we understand should be as irrelevant to us as is the fact that some human beings in relation to whom we have ethical obligations—severely retarded children, for example—can neither reason nor talk. Quoting Jeremy Bentham, the late eighteenth-century utilitarian philosopher, Singer writes, "The question is not, Can they reason? nor, Can they talk? but Can they suffer?" (Singer 1975, 8).

Singer's answer, of course, is yes. Not only do animals act as if they experience pain, he says, biology shows that the higher animals—other mammals, for example—are equipped with neurophysiological mechanisms for pain similar to our own. Because animals can suffer, we have ethical obligations not to inflict upon them more pain, relative to their capacities for sentience, than we would inflict on creatures of our own kind, relative to our capacities. We are obliged not necessarily to treat all creatures equally but, rather, to give all sentient creatures equal moral consideration (1975, 3). To neglect such consideration is to fall into a bias that is just as unacceptable in its own way, and analogously destructive in its consequences, as racism or sexism. Singer calls it "speciesism."

In helping us to move beyond speciesism, Singer proposes several forms of action. In addition to ending unnecessary experimentation in science and the unnecessary infliction of pain on animals in industry and agribusiness, we should end many other practices that society currently sanctions. For example, we should stop "hunting for sport or furs; farming minks, foxes and other animals for their fur; capturing wild animals (often after shooting their mothers) and imprisoning them in small cages for humans to stare at; tormenting animals to make them learn tricks for circuses, and tormenting them to make them entertain the folks at rodeos; slaughtering whales with explosive harpoons; and generally ignoring the interests of wild animals as we extend our empire of concrete and pollution over the surface of the globe" (1975, 23). We should write to our political representatives urging them to pass legislation that obstructs these activities; make our friends aware of the issues; educate our children to be concerned about the welfare of all sentient beings; and protest publicly on behalf of nonhuman animals (1975, 163).

Finally, Singer argues, we should become vegetarians. "Whatever the theoretical possibilities of rearing animals without suffering may be, the fact is that the meat available from butchers and supermarkets comes from animals who did suffer while being reared" (1975, 165). The people who profit by exploiting large numbers of animals on factory farms "do not need our approval. They need our money" (1975, 166). It is only by our boycotting meat that animals can cease to suffer under the conditions of contemporary factory farming.

From this it should be clear that animal rights advocates differ from land ethicists. Whereas land ethicists are systems-oriented, animal rights advocates are individual-oriented; whereas land ethicists are concerned with the stability, integrity, and beauty of ecosystems, animal rights advocates are concerned with the suffering of particular creatures; whereas land ethicists are concerned with the value of rivers and mountains, animal rights advocates emphasize other animals.

Must the biocentric Christian choose between these two traditions? I think not. The task instead is to synthesize aspects of each
into a larger whole: into a life-centered ethic that responds both to
the abuse of individual animals under human subjugation and to the
degradation of larger biotic wholes, which are themselves habitats
for countless living beings. Put differently, the task is to shift horizons in such a way that anthropocentrism with respect to individual
animals *and* ecological wholes is eliminated. To eliminate anthropocentrism is to recognize the intrinsic value of life.

II. The Intrinsic Value of Life

To be anthropocentric is to be centered in the human being to the
exclusion of other creatures. While a life-centered ethic is avowedly
nonanthropocentric, it need not imply that *all* types of anthropocentrism are inappropriate. At this stage in evolution, for example,
humans seem to be the only creatures who have the capacity for, and
responsibility to develop, a biocentric ethic. For the most part other
creatures seem not to have a capacity for the all-inclusive care that
rightly unfolds as a stewardship of the Earth and a care for all its
creatures. Nor do they have the need for an environmental ethic,
since they are not the primary cause of our shrinking forests, lost
topsoil, polluted air, contaminated water, and depleted ozone layer.
We human beings are the culprits. To recognize our uniquely human
responsibility and moral calling is to be appropriately anthropocentric. It is to exclude other animals from a responsibility toward
which, to the best of our knowledge, only we are called. Only humans
sin by not adopting a biocentric ethic.

This unique moral calling has important theological implications.
The human capacity for inclusive stewardship can be understood as
part of what it means to be made in the image of God. Biocentric
Christians can propose that God's image in human life is not a
warrant for arrogance but rather a potential for mirroring, in a finite
way and given human limitations, that reverence for life which is
God's own.

When advocating a transcendence of anthropocentrism, however,
it is not moral agency that is of concern to most animal preservationists and others interested in a biocentric ethic. Instead it is moral
patience, moral considerability. By "moral agency" I mean the act
of making moral decisions in relation to other beings. A moral agent
is a being (usually, but not necessarily, human) who has, or should
have, a conscience, and whom we hold responsible for his or her
decisions in relation to other beings. By "moral patience" I mean the
act of receiving ethical regard. A moral patient is a moral beneficiary:
that is, a being who deserves the respect and care of moral agents.

To be a moral patient is to be an end as well as a means. It is to have an intrinsic value that elicits care and respect from moral agents, that precludes moral agents from exercising certain forms of violence and manipulation, and that obligates those agents to act, as best they can, to facilitate one's well-being. Animal preservationists act, at least in part, because they recognize that nonhuman animals can be moral patients.

While some nonhuman animals may exemplify some degree of moral agency—as for example when elephants feed injured members of their own species, or when ducks adopt the young of other species, or when porpoises aid humans in distress—moral patients need not be moral agents. Christians and others have long recognized that many humans—the very young, the very old, the mentally handicapped, and the emotionally disturbed—are moral patients, even though they may not be, or have the capacity to be, moral agents. Despite the fact that some of these people lack an ability to reason, to use language, or to exercise moral agency, they seem to us important in their own right. We say that they cannot be treated simply as instruments for our purposes, that they are ends in themselves, that they must be treated with respect and care, that they cannot be abused or victimized. This is to say that they have intrinsic value.

But what is it about such humans that gives them their intrinsic value and their moral considerability? If we can identify that attribute in them which, despite their lack of moral agency and other assorted attributes, gives them intrinsic value, perhaps we then understand that attribute which, possessed by *any* creature, gives it such value.

The Intrinsic Value of Human Beings

Consider a physically and mentally handicapped two-year-old girl in a hospital whose family has died and whose potential service to society—by most criteria cherished in the society—is negligible. Imagine further that the hospital is understaffed and overworked, so neither nurses nor doctors are able to give her much time or care beyond that of physical maintenance. Though in principle she could be of instrumental value to them—in the sense that she might contribute to their lives through the sense of well-being they gain from serving her—they are too busy to partake of such enrichment. Her days are spent lying in bed, receiving care, and attending, as much as she can, to the sights and sounds around her.

Imagine that you—the reader—work in the hospital, and you walk in to see her, if only briefly because you too are overworked. As you look at her, you recognize that her "instrumental value" to other human beings is negligible. For a moment you wonder if it is worth the resources of the hospital, and perhaps even your own resources, to care for her. Nevertheless, as you look at her, you feel that she matters, that her life is important, that she should be cared for in her short duration on Earth, if at all possible. Without using the words, you have an intuition of her "intrinsic value," her value apart from her usefulness to yourself and to others. What is it about her that elicits this intuition?

You might say that she is a child of God, one of God's creatures. And from the point of view of this work, you would not be wrong. But these phrases are abstract; they are theological interpretations of that about her which elicits your intuition. As she lies before you, your intuition of her intrinsic value is not provoked by abstract theological claims. Rather, it is elicited by the very fact of her subjectivity, the fact that she is not simply an object for you but also a subject for herself. To experience her as having intrinsic value is to experience her as a kindred subject.

When we perceive the girl as a subject, we implicitly recognize two facts about her, facts that are essential features of her subjectivity and that make her a subject. These facts are that she has "value for herself" and that she has "value in herself." Let me explain what I mean by each of these two phrases.

To say that the girl has value *for* herself is to say that her existence is a matter with which she herself is concerned, that her life is important to her, that she matters to herself. To have value for oneself is not necessarily to think about oneself as having value, nor is it necessarily to enjoy positive self-regard. Rather, it is to have internal interests, or interests of one's own. For most people these interests are dimly discerned but deeply felt aims to live with some degree of satisfaction relative to the circumstances at hand. In the case of the girl, these interests would include an interest in being fed, in being warm when she is cold, in being allowed freedom of movement, and in being touched. The girl is a kindred subject because she has interests.

The girl's interests need not be felt *consciously* by her in order for them to be her own or in order for us to appreciate them. At least this is the case, given certain meanings of the word "consciousness." In common parlance the word "consciousness" often has one or both of two meanings. It can refer to focused perceptual attention on clearly defined data, as, for example, when I say, "I am now conscious of the tree outside my window." Or it can mean reflexive awareness, as when I say, "I am conscious of the fact that I am aware of the tree." Consciousness can mean (1) clear and distinct awareness of a perceptual or cognitive datum or (2) awareness of this awareness. Given either or both of these two meanings, interests need not be consciously felt in order to be one's own.

For example, in early evening, having last eaten five or six hours ago, the girl may have an interest in being fed. She need not experience this interest as an object of clear and distinct perception in order for it, and hence her own life, to matter to her. She may not be "aware of her awareness" of her hunger. Instead, like most of us, she may feel the interest as a dimly discerned, vaguely felt need: in this case a physical rather than a mental interest.

Whitehead spoke of such interests as *physical* purposes. These purposes include subconsciously apprehended goals and aims for relieving unpleasant sensations or for acquiring absent pleasures. *Mental* purposes, too, can be goals and aims. The actualizations of such aims involve distinctly psychological forms of satisfaction: as, for example, when the girl needs and receives affection. The point, however, is that aims or purposes, whether physical or mental, need not be consciously entertained in order to be important to humans. Wherever there is an internal need, physical or mental, apprehended either consciously or subconsciously, there is an interest. And wherever there is an interest, there is a kindred subject.

The second thing we recognize about the girl when we see her as a subject—in addition to the fact that she has value for herself—is that she has value in herself. The phrase "value in itself" can be defined in many ways. I use it to refer to experiential richness of a creature's life as lived from the inside. The girl has value in herself because she has experiences that have a qualitative richness—a value or goodness—in their own right. This is to say that in her own way the girl takes into account her own body and aspects of her environment from a unique point of view and that these acts of taking into account have, or can have, a qualitative beauty of their own as enjoyed from her own perspective. When she is fed, she tastes the food, and that taste has a pleasure of its own which is good; when she hears a sound and responds to it, her hearing has a harmony of its own which is good; when she feels the touch of another, she experiences that touch from her own point of view, and that experience has an intensity of its own which is good. The goodness—or qualitative richness—of these and other experiences may well be foreign to the forms of richness we ourselves enjoy. Nevertheless we sense its presence, and for that reason, as well as the fact that she has value for herself, we believe she has intrinsic value.

In order to have richness, the girl's experiences need not be conscious in the senses just defined. They can be bodily, or they can be psychological but dream-like. Most human experience is of the latter sort; it consists of dimly discerned and vaguely felt fantasies, reflections, memories, and hopes. It is similar to dream experience, in which we feel the presence of sounds and images, though not in a conscious way. While consciousness is a form of experience, not all experience is conscious. The girl is a subject because she has richness of experience, conscious or subconscious.

Generalizing from the example of this girl, I suggest that other people have intrinsic value because they are subjects with value for themselves and with subjective experiences that have value in themselves. Their experiences have a unique quality that, even if quite different from our own, can inspire our concern and often our appreciation. Their interests are the very ways in which their lives matter to themselves. "Intrinsic value" is a name for, and pointer to, the value other people have for themselves and in themselves. This intrinsic value is also valuable to God. God loves people not simply as instruments for divine purposes but as subjects with value in and for themselves. A Christian ethic will love other people as God loves them. It will love them for who they are and not simply for how useful they are. Before turning to God, however, we must first ask whether an ethic—Christian or otherwise—that recognizes intrinsic value should limit itself to people.

The Intrinsic Value of Other Animals

Might a nonhuman creature, too, have experiences and interests? And, if so, might it too have intrinsic value? As Bernard Rollin, author of *Animal Rights and Human Morality* (1981), points out, there is evidence from at least five sources to suggest that at least some other animals, particularly those with advanced nervous systems, are subjects with interests and experiences and hence with intrinsic value.

First, and particularly relevant to nonhuman animals with nervous systems, there is the evidence from neurophysiology. In Rollin's words, "the presence of a nervous system in an animal certainly suggests that these structures perform a function similar to that performed" in human beings (1981, 41). Just as, in human beings, nervous systems provide physical contexts for taking into account external stimuli in light of internally experienced interests, so must nervous systems function in other animals.

Second, there is biochemical evidence. "The presence in an animal of a biochemical mechanism that is similar to a mechanism in [human beings] that regulates some conscious state is evidence for something like that state in the animal" (1981, 41). Rollin points out that this principle may apply even to earthworms, in whom have been found the very chemicals (endorphins and enkephalins) that in human life are known to have pain-killing properties.

Third, there is behavioral evidence. "When an animal yelps or thrashes or shows avoidance behavior in the presence of a stimulus known to be harmful or unpleasant to [human beings], that is evidence for awareness in the animal" (1981, 41).

Fourth, there is anatomical evidence as manifest, for example, in the presence of sense organs. The existence of eyes, organs for hearing, organs for touch or taste "certainly suggests that an animal enjoys some kind of consciousness" (1981, 41).

Fifth, there is evidence from evolutionary theory. "Given that evolutionary theory is at the cornerstone of all modern biology, and evolutionary theory postulates continuity of all life," it is implausible "to suggest that a creature that has a nervous system displaying biochemical processes that in us regulate consciousness, or that withdraws from the same noxious stimuli as we do, or from other dangers, and that has sense organs, does not enjoy a mental life" (1981, 41). Better to assume the obvious: namely, that it too is a subject with experiences and interests.

Of course, these conclusions contradict the mechanistic understanding of nonhuman life that has prevailed in the life sciences since the seventeenth century. For the most part, twentieth-century biologists have bracketed altogether the question of animal awareness, or they have viewed animals as mere machines devoid of such awareness. Nevertheless, Rollin's conclusions are supported by a minority movement within contemporary biology called "cognitive ethology." Just as cognitive *psychologists* take as their task the study of the cognitive life of humans, so cognitive *ethologists* like Donald Griffin (1984) investigate that of nonhuman life. With the help of laboratory experiments and field work, they explore the kind of conscious intelligence involved, for example, in an animal's construction of a domicile, or its use of tools, or its involvement in predator-prey relations. They see consciousness as a means by which vertebrates and invertebrates are able to alter their behavior in order to deal with variables in their environments.

Let us assume that Rollin's arguments and the perspective of the cognitive ethologists are correct. This means that at least some other animals have intrinsic value. Three points can be noted about this value: points that apply to human and nonhumans alike.

The first is that an experiencer's intrinsic value—be it human or nonhuman—is objective in the sense that it exists independently of its being recognized by an external observer. It is not assigned or ascribed; it is recognized or discovered. Just as the girl in the hospital has value to herself and an experiential perspective of her own, whether or not others recognize it, so all subjects—human and nonhuman—have value to themselves and experiential perspectives of their own whether or not recognized by others. This objectivity is subjective in the sense that it is the subjective dimension of the being at issue. Yet the subjectivity is itself objective in the sense that it exists—with its own richness of experience and its own interests—independently of its being affirmed by others. An organism's intrinsic value is the organism's unassigned being-for-itself.

The second point is that an organism's being-for-itself, and hence its intrinsic value, is relational, which is to say that it is dependent on the causal influence of many other things. This may seem to contradict the point made earlier, but it does not. While an organism's subjective existence does not depend on the recognition of other actualities, it does depend on the existence, and hence the causal influence, of other entities. Subjective experience is itself a creative appropriation of such influences in light of interests felt by the subjective experiencer, and these influences affect the quality of the experience itself. Just as the quality of experience available to human subjects is partially dependent on the history by which those persons are shaped and on the environmental circumstances in which they find themselves, so the quality of experience available to nonhuman subjects is dependent on past and present realities. A young male deer in a forest is dependent on the evolutionary heritage from which he emerges, and on the plants he eats, the water he drinks, and the other deer with whom he exists in some sort of social relationship. Consciously or subconsciously, he takes into account sights, sounds, smells, and tactile sensations that enrich and gradually shape his own point of view. The quality of his own life, and the realizability of his own interests, would be seriously diminished if he were placed in a different, less variegated, setting. To be a reality for oneself—human or nonhuman—is to be dependent on, and affected by, other things, for good or ill. No organism, even from its own perspective, is an island.

The third point is that—amid its intrinsic value and its dependence on other things to support and enrich this value—an organism can also be of instrumental value to others. Consider the young deer. Even as he has value for himself, he also has value for others. He is an object of prey for other mammals, his feces nourish the soil in which worms and microbes live, his body houses parasites, and his eating habits maintain a balance of plant life. The deer is part of an ecosystem in which he plays an instrumental role. Even as he has intrinsic value, he has instrumental value.

III. The Practice of a Biocentric Ethic

As animal activists recognize, neither the instrumentality of an organism for other organisms nor the relationality of its own subjective existence belie the fact that it has intrinsic value, and hence that it is a moral patient. While there may be differences between human and nonhuman experiencers, no differences justify inclusion of the former and exclusion of the latter from moral considerability.

Does this mean, then, that animals have rights? If so, what about plants? And rocks? And mountains? And stars? In reconciling the concerns of animal rights activists with those of land ethicists, I believe it helpful at the outset to limit the use of the word "rights" to individual animals (1) who have discernible interests in living with some degree of satisfaction and (2) whose interests can be respected or violated by human moral agents. To say that these animals have rights is to say that we, as humans, have duties to respect their interests.

In advocating a Christian respect for animal rights, Christians have much to learn from Andrew Linzey, the Christian thinker who has done most to develop a theology of animal rights (1986; 1987). Still, the perspective I am developing differs from Linzey in one important respect. For Linzey, humans and other animals possess what he calls "theos-rights." Theos-rights are "concerned with the defence of God's given spiritual capacities exhibited within his creation and realized through his covenant relationship with them, and not with any capacities which may be claimed by the creature itself in defence of its own status" (1987, 83). Here Linzey disagrees with the philosopher Tom Regan, with whom he works closely. In *The Case for Animal Rights,* which is the most sustained philosophical defense of an animal rights perspective to be written in the latter decades of the twentieth century, Regan argues that being "subject of a life" is a sufficient criterion for the possession of moral rights (1983, 243–248). The biocentric Christian can agree with, and learn from, Regan on this matter.

Even if there were no God, individual living beings would deserve our respect; they would have rights. The role of God in a life-centered ethic is not to ground the rights of animals, as if their rights were assigned by God. Rather, the role of God is to beckon us into a respect for those rights, to lure us toward a care for animals that, in our own finite way, mirrors and internalizes God's own care.

In order to affirm this point, it can be helpful to imagine God on the analogy of a cosmic Parent. Imagine, for example, that the Psyche of the universe is in some way like a human mother, except that her love is utterly unfailing and unlimited. A human mother may in some sense create her children, but once the children are created, they have a goodness that is independent of her ascription. Even if she decides they are valueless, they nevertheless have value as living subjects with goals and needs of their own. Similarly, though God lures sentient beings into existence out of a primordial chaos, those sentient beings have a value that is independent of God's ascription. In Genesis, after creating the animals on the fifth day,

God does not assign them their goodness, God *sees* that they are good (Gen. 1:21). God is "God" because she invites others to share in her wisdom. She beckons us, humans made in her own image, to recognize the intrinsic value that she herself sees.

Nonhuman animals have rights because they have intrinsic value. Some of these rights apply primarily to animals under human domestication, to those we have brought into our own human communities through no choice of their own. Experimental rabbits, for example, have obvious interests in avoiding unnecessary pain, and their rights to happiness seem clearly violated by humans who subject them to pain in order to test consumer products such as mascara. This is not to suggest that rights are absolute, even for humans. A domesticated rabbit's right to satisfactory existence may be overridden if such is necessary for the survival of humans and other species. By this criterion, however, testing of eye makeup is *not* permissible since humans can survive without mascara. By contrast, testing of a life-saving vaccine is permissible if no other option is available. To say that a domesticated animal has rights is to recognize that we have duties to respect its interests in living with satisfaction, given its biological propensities, and that the burden of proof for violating these interests lies with us, not with the animal.

With respect to domesticated animals, the rights at issue are to life, liberty (e.g., freedom of movement), and the pursuit of happiness (e.g., freedom to avoid unnecessary pain and to enjoy desired subjective states). For the sake of convenience, these three rights can be called "individual rights." As is obvious to any naturalist, these rights do not apply to interactions between nonhuman animals, particularly those involved in predator-prey relations. Consider the rabbit being chased by the fox. It makes little sense to say that the rabbit's rights are being violated by the fox, because the very concept of "right" implies a moral agent whose duty it is to respect it. The fox chasing the rabbit is not a moral agent. Because the fox does not and cannot recognize its duty to respect the interests of the rabbit, it makes little sense to say that the rabbit has a right to have its life respected by the fox. Individual rights, while accruing to moral beneficiaries, are simultaneously dependent on moral agents who can respect them: that is, on human beings. In this sense rights are human-dependent. While their recipients are not limited to human beings, their effective functioning is dependent on human recognition.

Recognizing that rights are human-dependent, we might nevertheless wonder, albeit abstractly, if prey do not have rights to be protected from predators by humans. In some instances, of course, we do protect prey from predators: birds from cats, for example. But in general we recognize that the protection of prey from predators is impractical. Predators, too, have interests that are worthy of our respect, and yet the fulfillment of these interests necessarily involves a violation of the interests of the prey. If we protect the interests of the rabbit, we violate the interests of the fox, or vice versa. Cognizant that life itself has a tragic dimension—that "life is robbery," as Whitehead put it—we had best leave wild creatures alone. Our respect for animal rights applies primarily to animals under human domestication and to those we hunt.

Necessary as it may be to limit the recognition of individual rights to animals under human domestication, it is equally important to recognize that wild animals are "moral patients" and that they have other kinds of rights, such as the right to habitat protection. We may indeed have certain duties to wild animals—such as protecting their habitats and preventing the unnecessary extinction of their species—even if we do not apply the language of individual rights to them. The category of moral patience is itself more inclusive than that of individual rights.

Furthermore, it is important to recognize, as will be argued in greater detail, that there can be degrees of moral patience, or moral considerability. The greater the intensity of a creature's interests, the greater our obligation to respect them. Simple plants, for example, have interests, at least insofar as the cells of which they are composed have aims and needs. Yet the intensity of a plant cell's aim to survive—much less to survive with satisfaction—does not seem to be as great as that of a porpoise's interest in surviving with satisfaction. Instrumental considerations being equal, it is more problematic to take the life of a porpoise than a simple plant, which is to say that the porpoise has a greater degree of moral patience than the plant. While every living being has moral patience of one sort or another, some have more than others. A speculative justification for this claim, hinging on a structural difference between plants and animals and a recognition of degrees of intrinsic value, is offered in the final section of this chapter.

Finally, it is important to recognize that the category of intrinsic value is itself more inclusive than that of moral patience. Rivers, rocks, and stars may have intrinsic value, even though they are not moral patients with discernible interests subject to human violation. Many more things have intrinsic value than have rights. Indeed, biocentric Christians can affirm that all existents—inorganic as well as organic—have intrinsic value.

The speculative foundations for expanding the notion of intrinsic value beyond animals to plants and even rocks will be suggested shortly. For now, however, let us assume that a biocentric ethic should respect the rights to life, liberty, and the pursuit of happiness of individual animals under human domestication and the rights to habitat protection of living beings in the wild. What would it mean, then, to live in light of such respect? It would mean both that we adopt certain biocentric practices and that we embody what might be called biocentric virtues. First, consider some of the practices.

Biocentric Practices

Given the manifold areas in which humans abuse domesticated animals, we must practice a respect for animal rights on a case-by-case basis. In general, the following principles of the Humane Society of the United States (Morris 1978, 236) can serve as guidelines for appropriate action:

> It is wrong to kill animals needlessly or for entertainment or to cause animals pain or torment.
>
> It is wrong to fail to provide adequate food, shelter, and care for animals for which humans have accepted responsibility.
>
> It is wrong to use animals for medical, educational, or commercial experimentation or research, unless absolute necessity can be demonstrated and unless such is done without causing the animals pain or torment.
>
> It is wrong to maintain animals that are to be used for food in such a manner that causes them discomfort or denies them an opportunity to develop and live in conditions that are reasonably natural for them.
>
> It is wrong for those who eat animals to kill them in any manner that does not result in instantaneous unconsciousness. Methods employed should cause no more than minimum apprehension.
>
> It is wrong to confine animals for display, impoundment, or as pets in conditions that are not comfortable or appropriate.
>
> It is wrong to permit domestic animals to propagate to an extent that leads to overpopulation or misery.

As Birch and Cobb point out (1981, 156), "the serious application of these principles would enormously reduce the suffering now inflicted by us on our fellow creatures."

It is noteworthy that the principles of the Humane Society do not prohibit the killing of animals for food. However, contrary to John Henry Cardinal Newman (1801–1890), who argued that the least human good compensates for any possible cost to animals, biocentric Christians recognize that "it requires a great human advantage to compensate for animal suffering and loss" (Birch and Cobb 1981, 161). Despite the possible justification of killing animals for food in certain circumstances, particularly if necessary for human survival, Christians in industrial societies whose lives do not depend on the eating of meat can and should choose vegetarianism. Given the appalling conditions under which most animals are raised for food and transported to slaughter, we are right to follow Peter Singer's advice and boycott the meat industry.

This is not to say that cows, sheep, chickens, and fish have an *inviolable* right to life. Rather, it is to say that they have interests in surviving with some degree of satisfaction and that as moral agents we humans must be as sensitive as we can to these interests. The needs of animals to avoid unnecessary pain and to pursue pleasure are persistently violated by factory farming techniques such as the debeaking of chickens and the immobilization of veal calves. If we want factory farming abuses to end, we ought to boycott meat industries. In so doing, we can simultaneously serve the interests of the human poor, for, as Singer has argued, the adoption of vegetarianism helps reduce the waste currently involved in feeding grain to animals and thus helps encourage the production of crops more suited to the world's hungry. Vegetarian diets are also salutary for health reasons, since they are low in cholesterol and fats (Robbins 1987, 148–348). And they can contribute to the well-being of the environment. The intensive rearing methods of modern agribusiness, which we support with meat buying, often have disastrous effects on the environment in terms of the waste products they release into rivers and streams; and the raising of animals for food in Central and South America, much of which meat is imported to supply Western tables, plays a considerable role in denuding the Earth of its tropical forests (Robbins 1987, 363–373). Here the World Council's interests in affirming human well-being and the integrity of nature can be jointly served by the adoption of a vegetarian diet.

As land ethicists in the tradition of Aldo Leopold rightly point out, however, an exclusive focus on the rights of individual animals under human domestication does not go far enough if we are to dwell as benevolently as possible with our kindred creatures. A concern for animal rights must be complemented by a concern for land ethics: that is, for the well-being of biotic communities that serve as habitats for living beings. Christians are reminded by land ethicists that the recognition of moral considerability of other animals must result in a concern for terrestrial ecosystems and for the countless species in the wild whose home is the Earth.

Endangered species are themselves collections of individual beings that, if subjects, have intrinsic value and moral patience. Whether plant or animal, each member of a species embodies a form of life— that is, a distinctive way of experiencing with qualities of its own and with distinctive needs—characteristic of the species as a whole.

Among these interests is usually an aim for reproductive success and hence for the survival of at least some members of its own species. This form of life can be made into an object of reflection in its own right: something on the analogy of a Platonic form. But most proponents of a land ethic are not Platonic. They recognize that the form's actuality—that is, its life and vitality—is to be found only in the individual creatures that embody it. Preservationists are not interested in preserving the abstract form for its own sake, which could be accomplished simply by describing the form in books, perhaps with accompanying illustrations or photographs. Rather, they are concerned with preserving at least some of the individual creatures who embody that form. Here, too, the concern is with the intrinsic value and hence the moral patience of individual creatures. Many of these species, which include plants as well as animals, are endangered by pollution and by habitat disruption, which is itself partly the result of overpopulation and partly the result of a misuse and exploitation of land by ruling classes.

As in the case of animal rights, a Christian concern for species protection can seek to unite concerns for social justice with those for ecological sustainability. In Latin America, for example, the rural poor are often forced to farm the less arable land of tropical rain forests because the more productive land is owned by large agribusiness concerns. These rain forests are the habitats for many endangered species of plants and animals. If the arable land is reclaimed by the poor, their own poverty will be lessened, and the rain forests can themselves be better protected. Moreover, the forms of agriculture and land management traditionally practiced by rural peasants are often more conducive to ecological sustainability than are those practiced by absentee landlords. Christians rightly hope that policies and practices that promote social justice can also promote a respect for the integrity of endangered species.

In addition to working for modes of social justice that reduce the destruction of habitats, Lee Durrell in *State of the Ark: An Atlas of Conservation in Action* notes six practices many in industrial societies can adopt in order to help preserve habitats and the species threatened by their disruption. First, if we live in circumstances that allow, we can do our part to help minimize human overpopulation either by adopting children or by having children at replacement rate, two surviving children for every couple. Second, we can learn about the environments in which we live, trying both to understand the ecosystems of which we are a part and on which we depend and to advocate agricultural and industrial policies that are minimally destructive of those systems. Third, we can examine the consequences of our own professions and life-styles, adjusting our behavior where consequences are destructive of environmental well-being. Fourth, if we are among the affluent minority in the world, we can keep our consumption of new goods within reasonable levels, trying not to waste or overconsume water, energy, or food and learning to live more simply to allow for a more equitable distribution of the world's natural resources. Fifth, we can join environmental organizations oriented toward a protection of habitats and an ecologically sound use of resources. Sixth, if we are able, we can cast our votes for those legislators who promise to protect the environment and to respect the needs of individual animals under human subjugation (Durrell 1986, 215).

Moral Virtues

However, such practical steps are not enough if Christians are truly to overcome the anthropocentrism of our past. What is required, in addition to the taking of practical steps, is a conversion of sensibility and character. In general terms, to adopt a biocentric ethic is to be informed by three "moral virtues." Each of these virtues can be encouraged by local churches through education, liturgy, and worship, and each can be allowed to flourish in meditation and prayer.

The first moral virtue is reverence for life. This is to have an inward disposition that is respectful of, and caring for, other animals, plants, and the Earth and that refuses to draw a sharp dichotomy between human life and other forms of life. This reverence has been evident in primal traditions in Africa, Oceania, and the Americas, and in certain Asian religions such as Buddhism and Taoism. Christians in these nonwestern settings, as well as their sisters and brothers in the West, can well appreciate the fact that dialogues with other faiths can and should inform the development of a biocentric ethic.

The second moral virtue is *ahimsa,* or noninjury. This is to refrain as much as possible from the violation of other creatures' interests: for example, to refrain from inflicting pain when another creature has an interest in avoiding pain and to refrain from taking its life when it has an interest in surviving. The most dramatic example of this perspective as applied to nonhuman creatures is Jainism in India. The biocentric perspective developed by the World Council of Churches will not go as far as Jainism, but it can take this tradition as a welcome and ever-present challenge to the anthropocentrism that has prevailed in so much of Christianity.

The third moral virtue is the exercise of active goodwill. In relation to nonhuman creatures, this is not simply an avoidance of harm, it is the active fostering of opportunities for an animal to realize its interests. It is, for example, to protect and sometimes even to create habitats that are essential to the survival of a species and to provide individual animals under human domestication with adequate food and shelter.

For the Christian, each of these three virtues involves a generalization of the golden rule: an application of agape to neighbors who in many instances are nonhuman. The first of these three practices—reverence for life—is an art, not a science. In relation to nonhuman creatures, such reverence can and must be guided by factual information from biologists familiar with the anatomical and behavioral needs of the animal under consideration. But it also involves and requires imaginative empathy. Avoiding the extremes of anthropocentric projection on the one hand and an absolute denial of the sentience of other creatures on the other, one must imagine oneself inside the perspective of the creature at issue, experiencing the world from its perspective and in light of its interests. If this is impossible, as it is in many cases, one must at least imagine that the creature has an experiential perspective of its own informed by interests of its own. With regard to humans and nonhumans alike, imaginative empathy is an essential feature of a life-centered ethical perspective.

The second and third practices, noninjury and active goodwill, require capacities in addition to imaginative empathy: capacities of discernment and judgment. The kind of moral considerability appropriately given to a moral patient—human or nonhuman—depends at least in part on the kind of interests possessed by that patient. If an animal has an interest in being in a warm climate, that interest can and should be considered in one's treatment of it; if it has an interest in being in a cold climate, that interest should be taken into account. The interests to be considered by moral agents are those that are held by, or relevant to, the moral patient. Different patients have different interests.

Moreover, in a world where there are competing interests among moral patients, not all interests can be respected. We live in a world where life is robbery. For one creature to live, thus realizing its interests, others must die, thus having theirs frustrated. As humans, we too must choose between lives, violating the interests of some for the sake of respecting the interests of others. This fact becomes particularly relevant when we consider the intrinsic value—and hence the moral considerability—of nonhuman forms of life. Every time we wash our faces we kill millions of bacteria; every time we eat, we are accomplices in many deaths. As Gabriel Moran puts it, "To walk across the lawn, take a shower, or even to breathe is to assert that some human concerns outweigh some nonhuman concerns" (1987, 698). The discernment of interests involves and requires a recognition of competing interests and a ranking of interests. It requires judgment.

IV. Degrees of Intrinsic Value

The need for judgment—preceded as it must be by the recognition that all living things have intrinsic value—requires that a biocentric ethic be accompanied by an adequate theology of nature. While the existence of intrinsic value in nonhuman creatures does not depend on such a theology, the sustained recognition of such value does, as does the ranking of interests once intrinsic value is recognized. Consider two inadequate theologies of nature from which, in principle, Christians might proceed: the first obstructs the recognition of intrinsic value; the second obstructs any capacity to rank interests.

Two Inadequate Theologies of Nature

First, Christians can approach other animals with a mechanistic theology of nature that stems from seventeenth-century science. Animals are viewed as complex instances of lifeless matter in motion, different in kind from humans, who alone are thought to possess souls. Here animals become mere instruments for human or divine purposes. "Stewardship" means no more than prudent management of nonhuman "resources." The goodness of the earth and its creatures—a goodness of which Genesis speaks and which can be understood as that of intrinsic value—is ignored.

On the other hand, those disillusioned with a mechanistic orientation can approach other animals through the lens of an egalitarian monism, such as one finds, for example, in Taoist points of view or in the contemporary movement of Deep Ecology (Devall 1985). Such perspectives are often emanationist in orientation, pointing toward an ultimate stuff—God or the Tao—of which all things are expressions and on the basis of which all things have equal intrinsic value. These perspectives are indeed advances over a mechanistic orientation. With their help, we can recognize that we have something in common with the rest of nature because we are all expressions of the same ultimate reality. But if we follow the lead of such perspectives alone, we are left with no basis—other than arbitrary whim—for the kind of discernment and ranking of interests that is so needed if a biocentric ethic is to be practiced. When, for example, we must choose between the life of a ringworm-causing fungus and the interests of a dog whose skin cells and hair shafts are invaded by this fungus, egalitarian monism offers us no help in making the decision, since fungi and animals have equal intrinsic value. We may decide to take the life of the fungus, but we have nothing to say to others who choose the contrary. Nor have we anything to say to those who argue that the AIDS virus has greater right to life than the humans infected by it. Arbitrary whim is the final arbiter.

What is needed, then, is an adequate theology of nature. To be adequate, it must accomplish three tasks. First, it must help us see the reality and nature of subjectivity, and hence intrinsic value, in human as well as nonhuman life and then guide us in discerning how far down and across the evolutionary chain such value extends. It must deal with the reality, nature, and range of subjectivity. Second, it must help us distinguish types of organisms so that, among other things, we can deal with the world of plants as well as animals. And, third, it must help us distinguish degrees of intrinsic value.

Among the most promising of such perspectives to date is process theology, influenced as it is by biblical points of view and by the philosophies of Alfred North Whitehead and Charles Hartshorne. Consider the way process thinkers attempt to accomplish these three tasks.

The Reality, Nature, and Range of Subjectivity

Process thinkers suggest that subjectivity is as real as the physical world experienced by subjects and that there is intrinsic value wherever there is subjectivity. They propose, as I did earlier, that subjectivity is relational rather than atomistic, and they assert further that it exists not as something that endures over time but, rather, in discrete moments. From their perspective the life of an animal— human or nonhuman—consists of momentary subjective experiences that arise and then perish, to be succeeded by subsequent experiences that are influenced by them, and that also arise and then perish. The building blocks of an animal life—human included—are momentary occasions of experience. The animal subject does not have the experiences, as if the subject were one thing and the experiences another; rather, as is said in Buddhism, the subject *is* the experiences. The intrinsic value of the subject is the intrinsic value of its interest-laden experiences.

With regard to the extent of subjectivity, process theologians suggest that momentary subjectivity of the sort just described extends throughout the realm of nature, through living cells even into that "dead matter" of which living cells and inorganic materials are composed. They do not suggest that rocks and metal levers think or feel in ways similar to, say, human beings and other animals. But they do recognize, as do many quantum physicists, that at a submicroscopic level apparently solid bits of matter consist not of nugget-like particles but rather of vibrant, momentary pulsations of energy. And they aver, as do some quantum physicists, that each of these pulsations takes into account causal influences from its submicroscopic past in light of possibilities for appropriating those influences decided upon, by the pulsation itself, in the present To take into account a submicroscopic past—even if, as is probably the case, subconsciously—is to experience it in a primitive way. To do so in light of possibilities—even if the taking into account of those possibilities, too, is subconscious—is to have aims that in biological life we call interests. The speculative proposal of process theology is that what we call "pulsations of energy" at the submicroscopic level are the most primitive instance in our cosmic epoch of what later, in living beings, we call "occasions of experience."

Two Types of Organisms, Monarchies and Democracies

It follows from a process perspective that the entire cosmos is alive with subjectivity, with aims and interests, and hence with intrinsic value. All of nature's existents—from plants and bacteria to rivers and stars—either are intrinsically valuable or are aggregate expressions of energy events with intrinsic value. Christians can rightly affirm this along with process theologians, for it offers one way of recognizing the goodness of creation of which Genesis speaks. But the unqualified affirmation of such goodness leaves us with little guidance in ranking incompatible interests between organisms: say, those of a dog infected by ringworm and those of the fungus that has invaded its skin and hair shafts and thus caused the ringworm, or that of a cancer cell and that of a human being in whom the cell resides. In the case of the fungus and the dog, whose interests should the veterinarian respect, those of the dog or those of the fungus? If a theology of nature is to help us in making such decisions, it must offer us some way of distinguishing different forms of organization in which intrinsic value can be found, after which it might help us to discern different degrees of intrinsic value relative to these forms of organization. Here, too, process theology is helpful. Of the many forms of life on our planet, process theologians suggest there are at least two basic organizational types.

The first is called, metaphorically, a monarchy. While the atoms, molecules, and cells of a monarchically organized organism consist of billions upon billions of energy events, the organism is more than its body. It is also a psyche. This psyche is a presiding stream of pulsations—a dominant stream of experiences—each of which on occurrence consciously or subconsciously receives input from its body, initiating responses in its body to external stimuli. The psyche is the organism's spirit, its soul.

In organisms with complex nervous systems, the most intimate environment of the psyche is the brain. When we look at an organism's brain, we are not seeing the psyche; rather, we are seeing the physical context that nourishes that psyche. At any given moment the psyche itself is an occasion of experience, partly conscious and partly subconscious, that creatively synthesizes brain influences and, along with them, past experiences in the psychic stream and subjective aims derived from God. The momentary experience then affects subsequent brain and bodily activities.

As lived from the inside, these psychological states are the subjective unity—the being-for-itself—of the organism at that moment. The organism does not feel itself as isolated within a brain, cut off from the world by the boundaries of the body; rather, it feels itself as centered in a body and yet reaching out, with the help of its senses, to include the world within its grasp. The dominant occasion of experience is the lived experience of the organism; it is the organism as an embodied soul.

The other type of organism is a democracy. A democracy is a system of energy pulsations without a presiding psyche. It is a complex network of energy events without a dominant stream of experiences. As a totality of parts, a democracy is not a being-for-itself; rather, it is an aggregate of energy events, each of which may have being-for-itself. It is like a city in which all the agency and sentience lies with the individuals composing it. While this city may be more than the sum of its individual constituencies, it is not a "more" with experiences and interests of its own. A democracy *is* the totality of its parts in relation.

This typology helps us to distinguish plants and fungi on the one hand from animals on the other. Consider the dog infected by the fungus. She seeks food, shelter, variety in her environment. She tries to avoid pain, and she enjoys pleasure. Indeed, she seems quite capable of feeling affection for those who are kind to her and animosity or fear toward those who harm her. She is a psychophysical organism, a body with a psyche. In discussing her intrinsic value, we rightly focus on what we imagine to be her reality-for-herself as a psyche experiencing the world with the help of a body. We care for her body by feeding her, knowing that such feeding will make her, as a psyche, happier than she would otherwise be. We try to assure that she has an environment with variety, knowing that she, like us, can suffer boredom. A dog is a monarchy.[2]

By contrast, most plants and fungi are democracies. They are aggregates of cells without a presiding subject. The unity of the fungus infecting the dog's skin, for example, does not seem to exceed the unity of its cellular parts as parts. While the cells in the fungus may have interests in being nourished by chemicals in the dog's skin, there is little evidence that the plant as a whole has an experiential perspective of its own. Its interests are those of its cells as they exist in relation to one another (Cobb and Griffin 1976, 78). The fungus and most plants are democracies.

Of course, there are undoubtedly exceptions to these generalizations. More complex plants such as angiosperms may have the beginnings of a psyche, and less complex animals such as viruses may be more like higher plants. Furthermore, not all monarchies have the same degree of soul, the same strength of psyche. If they are monarchies, single cells probably have less soul—less strength of psyche—than multicelled animals, and multicelled animals with relatively simple nervous systems probably have less soul than those with complex nervous systems. Strength of soul is a measure of (1) the extent to which a given occasion of experience in a psychic stream is able to learn from previous experiences, thereby contributing to an ongoing identity over time, and (2) the extent to which, as it occurs, the subjective unity of a presiding experience has greater richness of experience than those of its component parts. On these criteria some organisms may have more soul than others.

With the help of this distinction between monarchies and democracies and the recognition that even among monarchies there are degrees of soul, the stage is set for the third function a theology of nature must accomplish: guidance in distinguishing degrees of intrinsic value and hence in ranking the interests of organisms.

Distinguishing Degrees of Intrinsic Value

Intrinsic value is the experiential richness and self-concern of an organism. If some organisms have greater intrinsic value than others, it must be because their experiences are richer and their self-concern greater. *Do* some organisms have greater experiential richness and self-concern than others?

Any answer to this question will be speculative, and it must be posed in humility. Yet speculation is required if we are to rank competing interests. If choices must be made between the interests of fungal cells and those of the dogs on whom they feed, or between the interests of malarial mosquitoes and those of the humans on whom they feed, we must try to respect the interests of the organisms with the greatest degree of intrinsic value: that is, with the richest experience and the greatest self-concern.

The only example of degrees of intrinsic value to which we have immediate access are our own lives. We know (1) that some moments of our own experience have greater richness than others, (2) that at some moments we matter more to ourselves than at others, and (3) that, in general, the greater richness of experience we have, or believe we can have, the more we matter to ourselves. Experiential richness and self-concern seem directly proportional. If we are to speculate concerning the degrees of intrinsic value in nonhuman organisms, we must assume that, in other creatures as well, there is a direct correlation between degrees of experiential richness and self-concern, and hence that those creatures that have, or can have, greater degrees of experiential richness also have, or can have, greater self-concern. Then we must seek criteria by which to evaluate richness of experience. And here our only option is to generalize from criteria discovered in our own experience.

Is such generalization warranted? I believe that it is. Within Christianity the very notion of creation—and the attendant claim that we are, like other animals, creatures of this creation—offers one resource for generalization. Whether understood metaphorically or literally, the second creation story in Genesis suggests that we and other creatures are made from the same earth: "The LORD God formed man of dust from the ground" (Gen. 2:7) and "out of the ground the LORD God formed every beast of the field and every bird of the air" (Gen. 2:19). The idea that we come from a similar substance suggests that we share features in common, among which might be general possibilities for richness of experience.

Adding to biblical perspectives is evolutionary theory, with its suggestion that there is an ontological continuity among and between life forms. On these grounds we rightly surmise that our own lives are instances of, rather than exceptions to, the phenomenon of life as it is found in other creatures. Just as our lives consist of occasions of experience with varying degrees of richness, so must their lives. This is not to deny that there is something distinctively human about human experience, just as there is something distinctively canine about canine experience and distinctively cellular about cellular experience. But it is to say that human experience, canine experience, and cellular experience are instances of a similar kind of activity: that of consciously or subconsciously taking into account environmental influences in light of consciously or subconsciously felt interests. And it is to say that amid this activity there is some kind of qualitative enjoyment, some kind of richness. We rightly surmise that the general qualities we find rich are those which, in different ways relative to the species at issue, other organisms find rich.

Let us identify first, then, the qualities we find rich. They are harmony and intensity. Each are affective tones qualifying our act of experiencing—that is, taking into account—influences from other beings.

Harmony is a general feeling of attunement, balance, accord, and affinity. For us, harmony often includes the attunement of our psyches with our bodies, or physical health. Amid such harmony, the "other beings" in relation to which harmony is felt are cells, tissues, organs, and limbs. Whether or not we enjoy health, harmony in human life can also be sought and enjoyed in relations with other people, with kindred creatures, with the world of ideas, and with God. Compassion, understood as sharing in the joys and sufferings of others, is one of the highest forms of harmony enjoyed by humans: a harmony that Christians claim mirrors God's own.

Intensity is zest or energetic vitality in relation to other beings. It is exemplified in feelings of creativity, energy, strength, excitement, enthusiasm, vigor, passion, and potency. In human life intensity has at least two forms: the active vitality of creatively synthesizing environmental, social, and historical influences and the receptive vitality of allowing oneself to be strongly affected by such influences. Active vitality includes the joy of artistic creativity and the zest of physical exercise; receptive vitality includes the immediate physical pleasure and the meaning found in allowing oneself to share in the sufferings of others. As the latter example suggests, richness of experience need not be pleasurable in order to be meaningful. Pleasure is one form of richness, but not all richness is pleasurable.

Can these two forms of richness—harmony and intensity—serve as criteria by which we evaluate, albeit speculatively, the richness of experience of other creatures? If divorced from aspects and associations that are uniquely human, and if applied with imagination and tentativeness, they can.

The creatures most distant from us and concerning which our speculations will have to be the most tentative are those molecular, atomic, and subatomic energy pulsations composing inorganic matter. We cannot know with assurance, but we can at least speculate, that in being drawn toward stable configurations, energy events are drawn toward certain forms of subconscious, submicroscopic harmony. Perhaps stability as observed from the outside is harmony as lived from the inside. And again we cannot know, but we can at least conjecture, that these harmonies are imbued with powerful intensities, as is evident from the release of energy when stable energy configurations are disrupted. No doubt these forms of richness would be subconscious and quite different from anything we know. Nevertheless, they would be primitive instances of what, later, we call richness of experience.

If in fact even inorganic realities enjoy certain forms of harmony and intensity, the moral stakes of this fact are not high. There is no evidence that the interests of inorganic materials at a submicroscopic level can be violated by human manipulation. This means that, in making moral decisions, inorganic materials can be treated as instruments for the well-being of plants and animals, humans included. While we may appreciate their intrinsic value—as, for example, when we feel the awesomeness of a mountain or the freshness of clean air—our appreciation of their intrinsic value is aesthetic rather than moral. Moral issues emerge when we consider the living beings for whom they serve as habitats.

When making moral decisions, ecosystems too can be treated

primarily as instruments for the well-being of the life forms they include. We respect the integrity, beauty, and stability of ecosystems not because these systems are agents or patients in their own right but, rather, because they include complex networks of living beings who are moral patients in their own right. The land ethic of which Aldo Leopold spoke, and which has fittingly captured the imaginations of so many in the environmental movement in the West, has its justification in a "life ethic," because land—understood broadly to include ocean and air as well as solid ground—is the habitat of life. We work to protect the Earth's lands, oceans, and atmosphere not because the interests of these inorganic materials can be violated but because living beings depend on them.

Though a land ethic has its value in serving a life ethic, speculations concerning the aliveness of "dead matter" are important because they help Christians affirm more deeply the goodness of the Earth, from which, after all, life itself emerged and on which life depends. Moreover, though the land and water masses composing the Earth may not command moral respect in the same way that, for example, other living beings command such respect, Christians can nevertheless enjoy religious awe in the presence of inorganic matter and its myriad forms, cognizant that we emerge out of matter's aliveness. From the living rock, after all, come the waters of spirit.

Somewhat closer to what we know as humans, but still requiring much tentativeness, are living cells existing in or outside the bodies of both plants and animals. Here the intuitions of a contemporary physician and writer such as Lewis Thomas in *The Lives of a Cell* can be helpful. Realizing that cells in our bodies have lives of their own, Thomas writes, "I like to think that they work in my interest, that each breath they draw for me, but perhaps it is they who walk through the local park in the early morning, sensing my senses, listening to my music, and thinking my thoughts" (1974, 2–3). Here Thomas, like many biologists, recognizes that living cells seem able to take into account influences from their environments and that, in so doing, they are drawn toward certain forms of energy exchange and balance. We cannot know, but we can at least speculate, that energy exchange and balance as observed from the outside are intensity and harmony as lived from the inside. As with the energy pulsations composing inorganic matter, the intensities and harmonies would be subconscious. And yet here, in contrast to energy pulsations, interests can indeed be violated. Cancer cells seem to have interests in surviving, and we violate these interests when we destroy the cells. The necessity of ranking interests among organisms becomes obvious.

Evolutionarily closer to our experience, and perhaps furthest from sheer speculation, are multicelled animals with psyches, or monarchies. As indicated earlier, evidence from neurophysiology, biochemistry, anatomy, behavior, and evolutionary theory shows that such animals have experiences and interests. By the same token we can conjecture that such animals enjoy, and are drawn toward, their own forms of harmony and intensity, either consciously or subconsciously. It is not difficult to imagine, for example, that at least subconsciously a butterfly enjoys a harmony of hunger satiation when it sucks nectar with its proboscis, or that a snake feels a subconscious intensity of physical movement when it strikes at a prey. Nor is it difficult to imagine that nonhuman mammals feel and enjoy experiential richness: for example, that a cat feels intensity while playing with other cats, that a chimp feels harmony when nursing her young, that a deer feels intensity when running through a forest, or that a dog feels harmony when satisfied by a meal. There is no need to say that such harmonies and intensities entirely transcend genetic influence or that they are divorced from bodily needs. On the contrary, opportunities for experiential richness may well be conditioned by genes and meet physical needs. But such physical grounding does not obviate the fact that these qualities of experience are enjoyed by the animal from its own perspective. Physically based or not, harmony and intensity seem to be the qualities desired, not simply by us but by those creatures closest to us.

With these speculative assumptions concerning living cells and multicelled organisms, we approach a basis upon which we can distinguish degrees of intrinsic value. If we assume a direct correlation between experiential richness and self-concern, organisms that on balance can enjoy greater degrees of harmony and intensity than those with which they are being compared will have greater intrinsic value. When we must rank interests, we can do so on the basis of such differences.

But this, of course, is theoretical. How can we decide *in fact* which organisms have greater intrinsic value? Here again we must generalize from human experience. We know that we are psyches supported by bodies, that some of our own experiences are richer than others, and that complex nervous systems are required for at least the kinds of richness of experience that we find most valuable. While some may propose that energy quanta or living cells enjoy forms of harmony and intensity that are equally if not more valuable than our own, we have no evidence for or against the claim. Lacking such evidence, and given the need for judgment in deciding which lives must be respected in cases of incompatible interests, we must act on the basis of what we do know from human experience. We can make concrete decisions on the basis of two assumptions: (1) that animals with psyches, or monarchies, are able to enjoy greater degrees of experiential richness and self-concern than are organisms without psyches, or democracies, and (2) that monarchies with more complex nervous systems are able to enjoy greater degrees of experiential richness and self-concern than those with simpler nervous systems. The first assumption implies that a dog has greater intrinsic value than a fungus, the second that a dog has greater intrinsic value than a tick.

Concerning these conclusions, however, two words of caution are in order. First, all creatures, monarchies or democracies, organic or inorganic, have some degree of intrinsic value. In a biocentric ethic, the spirit of land, water, and air—and that of single-celled organisms and plants—should be respected. Focused as it is on living beings, a biocentric ethic can and should be informed by an appreciation of the goodness of all creation.

Second, even when living beings are ranked in terms of their intrinsic value, it should be recognized that, from the nonhuman creature's own point of view, its own value is not less than those of other creatures we deem more valuable. As the tick invades the dog, it does not deem itself less worthy of survival than the dog. While in fact its life may matter less to it than does that of the dog to the dog, and its subconscious experiences may be less rich than that of the dog, it does not know this. A tick does not rank itself.

This truth must itself be internalized if humans attempting to practice a biocentric ethic are to avoid arrogance as we rank interests. The need for judgment on the basis of degrees of value must be complemented by reverence for life, and this reverence must itself involve empathy for organisms on their own terms. The practice of empathy can be fostered if it is recognized that such empathy has a cosmic counterpart in God. This is to say that there is an ultimate point of view—a divine perspective—in which each creature is appreciated on its own terms and loved for its own sake. Creatures with lesser intrinsic value may or may not contribute less to the divine perspective than creatures with greater value; in any case they are not loved less. For those interested in a biocentric Christianity, God must be conceived as loving all creatures on their own terms and for their own sakes: the living cell, the mosquito, the pelican, and the human being. In the previous chapter I showed how God could be thus conceived. In this chapter I have outlined some of the ethical implications of such a conceptuality.

3

A Life-centered Spirituality

If we move toward a biocentric way of thinking about God such as that proposed in the first chapter, and if we adopt a biocentric ethic such as that proposed in the second chapter, we will need, in addition, a biocentric spirituality. By "spirituality" I mean an inner sensitivity to, and embodiment of, religious values. By "biocentric spirituality" I mean a spirituality that includes among its religious values a celebration of life on Earth. A biocentric spirituality is important because it can undergird a biocentric ethic and because it is one way of communing with God.

Among the different sensitivities encouraged in traditional Christian spiritualities are an awareness of God within the depths of the self, communication with God as a holy Thou, and love of God through service to other people. A biocentric spirituality can recognize and value these traditional Christian sensitivities, and it can partake of the various disciplines—meditation, prayer, fasting, study, simplicity, solitude, service, and worship—that nurture them. In addition, however, it will emphasize three modes of awareness that directly pertain to our interactions with nonhuman nature. These are (1) a feeling for the organism, (2) a feeling for matrices, and (3) an awareness of what Buddhists call "Emptiness" as an enrichment of the first two feelings. The purpose of this chapter is to discuss these three dispositions.

While my explanation of these three sensitivities is theological rather than historical, it is important for Christians to recognize that the first two have important precedents in the Christian heritage. As H. Paul Santmire points out in *The Travail of Nature: The Ambiguous Ecological Promise of Christian Theology*, the first intuition—a feeling for the organism—has a unique and signal exemplar in Francis of Assisi, who saw living creatures as centers of value in their own right (1985, 106–119). And the second—involving as it does an openness to the Earth—has predecessors in Irenaeus and the later

Augustine, both of whom, in drawing upon biblical motifs of divine fecundity and migration to a promised land, celebrated the world of the flesh as both created by God and redeemed by God (1985, 31–60). Classical Christian attitudes toward nature may be, as Santmire puts it, "ambiguous" in their ecological promise, but there are, amid the ambiguity, bright spots from which contemporary Christians can rightly learn.

I. A Feeling for the Individual Organism

The phrase "feeling for the organism" comes from Barbara McClintock, the Nobel laureate who pioneered discoveries in gene transposition through years of work with corn plants. In a recently published biography, Evelyn Fox Keller describes McClintock's approach to these plants and in so doing reveals aspects of McClintock's understanding of nature. As she studies her corn plants, we are told, McClintock brings with her not simply the observational and analytical skills characteristic of all good scientists but also a certain kind of intuitive sensitivity, an inward openness to kindred creatures. McClintock tells Keller that, in good biological research, a person must have the patience to "hear what the material has to say to you," the openness to "let it come to you." Above all, she says, one must have a "feeling for the organism" (quoted in Keller 1983, 200).

What is this feeling? Judging from McClintock's comments and Keller's commentary, it is an appreciative and intuitive apprehension of an organism in three of its aspects.

In the first place, it is a feeling for the organism as a *unique individual.* "No two plants are alike," McClintock tells Keller, "they're all different, and as a consequence, you have to know that difference" (Keller 1983, 198). McClintock continues: "I start with the seedling, and I don't want to leave it. I don't feel I really know the story if I don't watch the plant all the way along. So I know every plant in the field, I know them intimately, and I find it a great pleasure to know them" (1983, 199).

In the second place, it is a feeling for the organism as a *mysterious other.* Keller quotes Einstein as saying that science often proceeds from "a deep longing to understand even a faint reflexion of the reason revealed in the world," but then she tells us that on this point McClintock may differ. "McClintock's feeling for the organism is not simply a longing to behold the reason revealed in this world." Rather, it is "a longing to embrace the world in its very being, through reason and beyond." And how does the organism supersede reason? "For McClintock, reason—at least in the conventional sense of the word—is not by itself adequate to describe the vast complexity—even mystery—of living forms. Organisms have a life and order of their own that scientists can only partially fathom" (1983, 200). This life of its own is the organism's otherness, and the intuitable and yet ungraspable elusiveness of this life is the organism's mystery.

In the third place, McClintock's feeling for the organism is a sensitivity to the creature as a *kindred subject.* Keller writes that "over the years a special kind of sympathetic understanding grew in McClintock, heightening her powers of discernment, until finally, the objects of her study have become subjects in their own right" (1983, 200). These objects "claim from her a special kind of attention that most of us experience only in relation to other persons." In fact, as Keller explains (1983, 200), the natural objects are not simply "objects" for McClintock, they are "organisms."

> Organism is for her a code word—not simply a plant or animal ("Every component of the organism is as much of an organism as every other part")—but the name of a living form, of object-as-subject. With an uncharacteristic lapse into hyperbole, McClintock says: "Every time I walk on grass I feel sorry because I know the grass is screaming at me."

Judging from Keller's assumption that McClintock's comment concerning walking on grass is hyperbole, we can perhaps infer that the quality of a corn plant's life-for-itself—that is, its life as a subject—would be markedly different from that of a human's life-for-himself or -herself. Compared to human subjectivity, corn plant subjectivity would undoubtedly seem mysterious in its otherness. Yet McClintock's orientation suggests that humans can feel a sense of kinship amid this mystery because, after all, humans and other living beings are jointly subjects. Corn plants are distant, perhaps very distant, cousins: strange and yet lovable kin.

If we assume that McClintock's sensitivities are genuine and that organisms are, in fact, strange kin to which we can be sympathetically attuned, we can understand McClintock's "feeling for the organism" as a mode of spirituality. It is an act that approximates God's own way of feeling the world, an act of feeling the world, as best one can, as God feels it.

Of course, this human sensitivity will differ from God's feelings in that, for God, an organism is not "other" in the sense of being something outside the divine life. Nor is it "mysterious" if by that word we mean "difficult to understand." If corn plants are for us distant cousins, they must be for God much closer relatives, perhaps best friends, even lovers. We see through a window dimly.

Still, from the perspective developed in this work, God does indeed have a feeling for the organism in that God feels it as a unique individual (or, as in the case of plants, an aggregate of individuals) and as a subject (or an aggregate of subjects). When we have a parallel feeling, however dim compared to God's, we approximate the divine mode of perception and share in it. We allow God to see the world—no, to feel the world—through our eyes and intuitions. We put on the mind of God.

For some, this feeling may be more easily enjoyed in relation to animals than plants. Indeed, some of us may know this feeling only in relation to pets. As a general rule, the closer an animal is to us on the evolutionary scale, the more able we may be to feel it as a unique individual and kindred subject. To date, little attention has been given by spiritual guides to methods for extending sympathy beyond our ordinary abilities to creatures from whom we are more distant on the evolutionary scale. As a first step, perhaps our own capacities for putting on the mind of God can be extended by observation and study, through which we discover the amazing complexity of even the simplest of organisms, and by meditational techniques, which enable us to empty our awareness of mechanistic preconceptions and simply look. To study corn plants for a long time, through books and in the field, and then to sit with one, watching it with unhurried patience, might help us to have that "feeling" that, at first, we may enjoy only in relation to companion animals.

Why attempt to develop capacities for such feeling? In the first place, a feeling for the organism is enjoyable in its own right. It is one aspect of that richness of experience toward which we are beckoned by the lure of God. As we enjoy the presence of other creatures, we mirror and internalize divine empathy for individual creatures, sharing in the joy that God herself must feel in her embrace of creation. We feel connected to the organism, which is one aspect of the harmony that, when combined with intensity, yields the fullness of life for us and for God.

In addition, however, a feeling for the organism has instrumental value, for it can serve the interests of a biocentric ethic. In chapter 2 I argued that the practice of a life-centered ethic involves an inward disposition that is respectful of, and caring for, the creature at issue. This feeling for the organism is that inward disposition. If arrogance is to be avoided, the ranking of interests that the practice of a life-centered ethic must involve is best undergirded by a nonjudgmental "feeling for the organism" that appreciates the mysterious otherness of an organism on its own terms.

II. A Sensitivity to Biotic Communities

A feeling for the organism mirrors and internalizes divine empathy for the individual creature. Yet just as divine love has breadth as well as depth, so a biocentric spirituality can and should have breadth as well as depth. Even as we attend to individual creatures on their own terms, we can attend to those broader matrices of which they and we ourselves are parts, and on which both we and they depend. In a biocentric spirituality, a feeling for the organism can and must be complemented by a feeling for networks, systems, or matrices. It must be complemented by a concern for what Aldo Leopold called "the integrity, stability, and beauty" of biotic communities (1949, 224–225).

There are, of course, many matrices for which we can have feelings. First, there is God herself, who is that living Matrix within whom all things arise and perish as parts of her own body. She is the dynamic and ever-evolving Whole of wholes, or, to use the language of Rosemary Radford Ruether, the Matrix of matrices (1983, 68–71). We are indeed within this Matrix, and there are various ways in which we can sense her presence. Whenever we gaze into the heavens, for example, and sense that we are part of an unimaginably vast network of stars and planets, we sense the presence of God, for she is indeed the adventure of the universe as One. We are implicitly aware of the divine Matrix when we are awed by the cosmic context of our lives, when we are struck by the fact that we are but citizens of a small planet in a backwater galaxy, and when we recognize that there may well be forms of life on other planets in our own galaxy or in other galaxies. If or when we come in contact with extraterrestrial forms of life, they too would deserve our moral consideration; they too would be recipients of a life-centered ethic. In any event cosmic awareness, understood as an awareness of the Matrix of matrices, needs to be an integral part of a biocentric spirituality. As Thomas Berry puts it, the universe itself is the "primary sacred community" of which we are a part (1987, 38). Our own actions and those of other living beings are themselves activities of the universe becoming conscious of itself through the phenomenon of life (Berry 1987, 37; 1988, 195). A biocentric spirituality may be centered on life in terms of its ethical commitments, but it can also be attuned to the cosmos of which it is an expression.

We are also implicitly aware of the divine Matrix when we consciously or subconsciously presuppose an ultimate context, or point of view, in which an event concerning the past is known for what it was, even though it has been forgotten, distorted, or neglected by human knowers in the present. For God is a living Whole in whose ongoing experience the past is included, such that, even when forgotten by us, it remains known. Whenever we attempt to recover and hence discover the past, we are attempting to plumb the depths of divine memory. Those whose histories have been ignored or distorted by a dominant class of historians, and who therefore search for their own roots, are themselves lured by God to discover God. They are drawn to remember things that people in power may have forgotten or obscured but that are capable of partial though meaningful recovery because, even if forgotten on Earth, they have remained vivid and capable of recollection in the adventure of the universe as One, in that collective memory I have called "the divine Heart." In sensitive, honest historical memory, as well as in cosmic awe, we dwell with, and implicitly sense the presence of, the divine Matrix.

In addition to God as Matrix, however, there are numerous other wholes to which we can be attuned in a biocentric spirituality. These include galaxies and the celestial spheres, the Earth, the family of life on Earth, ecosystems, communities, families, bodies (including our own), living cells, molecules, atoms, and subatomic complexes. Many of these wholes are themselves parts of other wholes, and many are composed of parts that are themselves wholes. The universe as a whole seems to be a divine Matrix consisting of matrices that are themselves composed of, and constitutive of, other matrices. Let us call these nondivine matrices "matrices" with a lowercase "m," as distinct from God, who is the universal "Matrix" with an uppercase "M."

To have a feeling for matrices is to be able to see things and to feel things as webs or networks, as systems of interconnectedness. Sometimes this feeling is simply an appreciation of other things as they exist in relation to one another and in relative independence from us. It may be to appreciate the way in which acacia trees depend on ants to ward off predators, or the way in which water depends on certain configurations of hydrogen and oxygen to form its consistency, or the way in which the moons of Jupiter depend on the planet's gravitational pull for their orbits. To have a feeling for matrices is to be sensitive to the instrumental value that some things can have for others and to the intricate complexity of these instrumental connections.

At times, however, our sense of connectedness involves an awareness of our participation in, and essential connection to, observed matrices. Here we recognize that we participate in matrices greater than ourselves: networks that include our families, our communities, our cultural heritages, our nations, the family of life, the solar system, the galaxy, or the cosmos. We cannot and should not absolutize these matrices at the expense of others or, to say much the same thing, at the expense of God. But we can appreciate them, and our own connections with them can be opportunities for realizing that richness of experience, that fullness of life, toward which God continually calls us.

Of course, not all connections with matrices are healthy, and sometimes we are called by the divine Mother away from matrices in which we are situated. This is particularly the case with human communities. Given the realities of economic inequity and political repression, the social networks to which we feel bound by birth or circumstance are often destructive rather than constructive of our own well-being and that of others. We find ourselves in communities, in social wholes, that must be transformed if they are to be hospitable habitats for humanity. We rightly attempt to create more wholesome social matrices for ourselves and others and, amid our quests, to enjoy connections with existing matrices that better nourish both us and the divine Mother.

One existing matrix with which we can enjoy connections as we work toward justice is the Earth itself or, as the Greeks spoke of her, Gaia. On the one hand, this enjoyment can involve a recognition that we are evolutionary participants in a web of life: an intricate network of producers (plants) and consumers (animals), habitats and species, through which energy and services are exchanged by us, through us, and within us. Amid this recognition we can be sensitive to the various life-support systems—such as the interlocking cycles of carbon, oxygen, carbon dioxide, and nitrogen—on which we are utterly dependent. Mindful of Rachel Carson's haunting and prophetic observation in *Silent Spring* that in many areas "the early mornings are strangely silent where once they were filled with the beauty of bird song" (1970, 97), we can take heed of the manifold ways in which today we threaten and disrupt these systems through intensive farming and grazing, resource depletion, urbanization, and pollution. We can see how important it is, as the International Union for the Conservation of Nature and Natural Resources urges, that we maintain essential life-support systems, preserve genetic diversity, and ensure sustainable use of species and ecosystems. A recognition of our dependence on the Earth can enable us to exercise that kindly use, that nondominating stewardship, toward which biblical traditions call us.

In addition to an intellectual recognition of our rootedness in the Earth, however, a biocentric spirituality can also involve a sensual—indeed, an erotic—love of the Earth, cognizant of the fact that the Earth is God's body. In feeling drawn toward healthy soil—enjoying its touch, its smell, and its visual appearance—we caress the very God whose body is that soil. In breathing clean air—enjoying the sensation of inhalation and exhalation—we breath the very God whose body is that air. In drinking clean water—enjoying its freshness against our palates—we drink the very God whose body is that water. And in journeying into the wilderness areas—feeling the pulsations of life unmanipulated by humans—we journey into the very God whose body is that wilderness. As our senses join soil, air, water, and wilderness, they join God. A biocentric spirituality can be a spirituality of touch, sound, and smell as well as thought. It will allow the senses themselves to be occasions for spiritual joy, and it will see spirit as immanent within, rather than cut off from, matter and flesh.

It is important to emphasize that a sense of connectedness with the Earth cannot and should not replace our yearnings for justice in human societies. In a biocentric context that is Christian, the quest for ecological sustainability can and must be part of a quest for social justice, with justice understood as economic equity for those who now suffer from poverty, political participation for those whose voices are not now heard, and a respect for personal liberties for those whose basic rights have been denied. Yet it is through a joyful connection with the Earth, a love of Gaia, that we can find inner resources for that transformation of human society that is so sorely needed in our time. As the American naturalist Alicia Bay Laurel puts it, "When we depend less on industrially produced consumer goods, we can live in quiet places. Our bodies become vigorous; we discover the serenity of living with the rhythms of the Earth. We cease oppressing one another" (quoted in Partnow 1977, 497).

As we awaken to the Earth of which we are a part and to the ecological matrices by which we and other creatures are sustained, two things become clear. First, no matrices are self-contained. All are relational in that they depend on the parts of which they are composed and on wholes external to their own boundaries. Even ostensibly "closed" ecosystems—such as tropical forests and coral reefs—are dependent on inputs from other ecosystems. While forests generate some of their own precipitation, they also rely on rain from storms that gather moisture and air from the oceans; while coral reefs seem relatively self-enclosed, they are fertilized by the feces of fish that return to the reefs to rest after feeding in distant beds of sea grass. No matrices are islands unto themselves.

Second, most of these wholes are dynamic rather than static. For example, individual ecosystems on Earth—whether in oceans, marshes, deserts, or forests—have themselves evolved, and their futures are to one degree or another open. Though for a time they may seem to endure and persist in stable fashion, their stability is maintained by a dynamic interplay of predator-prey relations and by a continual adaptation on the part of living organisms to environmental circumstances. All matrices—even the apparently stable ones—are instances of Heraclitan flux.

III. An Awareness of Buddhist "Emptiness"

Among the religious traditions of the world, the two insights just mentioned—that all earthly realities are interconnected and that all are in perpetual flux—have been most deeply realized in Buddhism. Buddhists have understood more deeply than Christians the inescapable ultimacy of interrelatedness and impermanence. Indeed, they have seen that, in addition to God, there is another kind of "ultimate," itself related to interrelatedness and impermanence, called Emptiness, which can serve as a foundation for an ecological ethic. Christians seeking a biocentric spirituality can well learn from Buddhism in this regard, though, as might be guessed, the suggestion that there is another "ultimate" can come as quite a challenge. Let us look first at how this challenge from Buddhist Emptiness may be met at a theological level, after which we will turn to the particular lessons to be learned.

Emptiness and God

Among a creative minority of Christian theologians in the United States, Europe, Japan, and Southeast Asia, an intensive dialogue with Buddhism has been occurring since the middle of the twentieth century. The dialogue with Zen Buddhists—upon which I focus in this chapter, primarily because it is that with which I have had most experience—has been centered for the most part in the United States and Japan, featuring luminaries such as D. T. Suzuki, Thomas Merton, Masao Abe, and John Cobb.

As Christians enter into dialogue with Buddhists, it is natural for both parties to search for commonalities, to hope that, after all, our ultimate concerns coincide. I have myself been in intensive discussions with Zen Buddhists over the years, in one instance with a philosophically inclined Zen Buddhist master for whom I served as an English teacher. In these discussions I—like other Christians, I am sure—have wanted to conclude that what Zennists mean by Emptiness and what Christians mean by God are one and the same. I have sought the security of discovering, after all, that the truth implicit in faith in God is identical to the truth discovered when one awakens to Emptiness. I have wanted it to be *true* that "the truth is one while the paths are many."

Despite my initial desires, however, the reality of dialogue has led me to different conclusions (see McDaniel 1984a; 1984b; 1985). The more I have talked with Zen Buddhists, the more it has seemed the truths to which they have awakened are different from those which enliven Christian faith. Discussions between Masao Abe (1985) and John Cobb suggest the same.

Abe and Cobb have come to recognize that the ultimates of their two traditions—Emptiness for the Buddhist and God for the Christian—are different. When Abe claims that his religion is centered around the ultimacy of Emptiness and Cobb that his is centered around the ultimacy of God, they have each come to realize that "Emptiness" and "God" are not simply two names for the same truth. Instead, Emptiness seems to be a name for one kind of truth and God for another.

Here, however, an interesting and hopeful possibility emerges for Christians eager to learn from Buddhism. If Buddhists are right to affirm the ultimacy of a transpersonal and nonteleological Emptiness, and if Christians are right to affirm the ultimacy of a personal teleological God, there may indeed be two truths, two ultimates to which these different paths lead. It is not as if Buddhists have been wrong about Emptiness and Christians right about God, or that Christians have been wrong about God and Buddhists right about Emptiness. Perhaps, on the contrary, both have been right.

This is what Cobb and other process thinkers propose (Cobb 1977; 1982, 86–90; Suchocki 1982, 155; Nobuhara 1983, 81–86). They suggest that both Emptiness and God are real, albeit in different ways, and that they are different types of realities around which a religion can be oriented: different types of ultimates. Though the Christian life is centered in God, Christians can learn from what Buddhists say and realize about Emptiness. And though the Buddhist life is centered in an awakening to Emptiness, Buddhists can learn from what Christians (and other monotheists, Jews and Muslims among them) say and realize about God. In so doing, of course, participants in both traditions will be creatively transformed in their respective self-understandings, though not in a way that forces Christians to abandon faith in God or Buddhists to abandon an awakening to Emptiness. Christians will become buddhized, and yet remain Christian, and Buddhists will become christianized, all the while remaining Buddhist.

In order to understand how it is possible for a Christian to recognize two ultimates, recall the discussion of God in the first chapter. In discussing relational panentheism, I suggested that God and the universe (in one form or another) have coexisted from a beginningless past through a limitless series of cosmic epochs. I proposed that, in our cosmic epoch, beginning as it did with a big bang ten to twenty billion years ago, the finite creatures forming the universe were at one time nothing more than a vast chaos of creative energy events not yet lured into physical order, much less biological life, by God. With the help of creaturely freedom, I submitted, God created the world not out of an uncreative nothing but, rather, out of a creative chaos.

If one accepts the idea that God created the world out of a preexisting chaos, which itself may have devolved out of previous forms of order, it follows that God does not have, and never has had, an absolute monopoly on creativity. Rather, God *and* the finite, momentary creatures composing the universe (be that universe in a state of relative chaos or relative order) have forever been expressing a similar though differentiated vitality: namely, the creativity to actualize possibilities for responding to influences from others, including one another. In a given entity at a given moment, say a pulsation of energy within the primal chaos of our cosmic epoch, this power is not a mere property among properties. It is the very essence, the innermost creativity, of the electronic pulsation: an act of spontaneous freedom by which—in responding to and integrating influences from its submicroscopic environment—the pulsation creates itself and, perhaps, responds to God. Then and now, self-creativity seems to be the very "stuff" of which an entity consists—albeit an empty or nonsubstantial stuff, since, as an act of individualized self-actualization, it is a spontaneous happening rather than a thing. As the essence of God and of each and every existent in the universe, and yet as empty of substantiality, this spontaneity is what Buddhists mean by Emptiness. At least this is what Cobb claims, and I with him.

It is important to recognize that Emptiness *as such* does not compete with God, though finite instances of Emptiness can and do diverge from divine aims. Considered in itself, Emptiness is neither an agent nor a patient, which is to say that it makes no decisions, has no purposes, and enjoys no feelings. Indeed, apart from its actualizations, Emptiness is more like a nothing than a something: a nothing that is perhaps rightly termed Emptiness or, as Masao Abe speaks of it, absolute Nothingness. This no-thing-ness is not a mere privation of being, a vacuous nothingness. It is a ground of sorts, for it is that of which all actualities are expressions. But it is a groundless ground, for it is in no way "more real" than its manifestations (Abe 1985, 158). It does not create beings or produce beings, as if it stood over against beings. Nor does it lure beings or beckon beings. Rather, it *is actualized* by beings, or, better, it *is* the activity by which beings *actualize themselves* in relation to one another. Abe puts it this way: "Everything in the universe, including you and me, is Empty and is in Emptiness. . . . This means that everything is respectively and equally limited or determined *by itself*" (1985, 162; Abe's emphasis). Abe speaks of this self-determination as "freedom." He sees such freedom as the very way in which, in a given entity, Emptiness is realized. Emptiness does not create freedom, Emptiness is freedom: the freedom of each and every worldly being in the universe and, so the Christian will add, the freedom of God.

It is important for us to note that sometimes these acts of freedom occur in ways that are beneficial to life and sometimes in ways that are destructive of life. This means that Emptiness is the freedom of Jesus and that of the Nazi, the freedom of the Buddha and that of the rapist, the freedom of God and that of Satan. In this context the word "freedom" should not connote something positive. At root, Emptiness is self-actualization as such, neither good nor evil but capable of being expressed as either or both.

If Emptiness is the ultimate reality, what kind of ultimate, then, is God? More often than not, "God" in the Western monotheistic traditions has named *an instance* of creativity rather than creativity as such. In particular, at least in Christianity, "God" has named that supremely creative being who called the world into existence, whose love for the world is unlimited, who calls humans into the fullness of life through love and justice, and whose hope is that all life be redeemed. God, then, is not the ultimate reality of the universe but rather the *ultimate actuality:* that is, that supremely sentient being by whom all other actualities can be drawn into the fullness of life on Earth and, as argued in the previous chapter, redemption following death.

In the past, it seems, most Christians in the world have tried to center their lives around God as the ultimate actuality, and many Buddhists—at least those of the nontheistic variety—have tried to center their lives around Emptiness as the ultimate reality. The key word in Christianity has been faith, which is trust in the God of love. The key word in Buddhism has been enlightenment, which can be understood as awakening to cosmic Emptiness. This does not mean that God has not been present in the lives of Buddhists. On the contrary, inasmuch as Buddhists have been drawn toward love and hope as an expression of their awakening to Emptiness, they have indeed been drawn by God. Nor does it mean that Christians have not expressed, and perhaps in some unthematized way known, Emptiness. Indeed, certain mystical traditions in Christianity seem to have awakened to Emptiness as the ground of God, calling Emptiness "the Godhead." To say that Christianity and Buddhism have been centered in different ultimates is to say, however, that in general the two religions have thematized different aspects of lived experience—Emptiness on the one hand and God on the other—as primary centers of religious orientation. In the future, so process theologians suggest, Christians might learn to recognize the truth of Emptiness even as they are centered in God, and Buddhists might learn to internalize faith in God even as they have awakened to Emptiness.

A biocentric Christianity can follow this proposal and try to include, within its own Christian ambience, insights and intuitions that mirror a Buddhist understanding of Emptiness. Of course, truly to realize Emptiness in a Zen context, one must undergo extensive meditation under the tutelage of an enlightened Zen master. In the Rinzai tradition at least, one must have the satori experience. Desirable as this might be, it is doubtful that large numbers of Christians will do this, though those with time and inclination can and should.

Large numbers, however, can get a feel for Emptiness by study and meditation. Amid study and meditation, they will discover that Buddhists have seen deeply into three aspects of Emptiness besides those mentioned above: aspects which, if at least partially intuited by Christians, can profoundly enrich a biocentric spirituality. Buddhists have seen, and Christians can try to understand, (1) that Emptiness, or ultimate reality, is suchness; (2) that it is *pratitya-samutpada,* or dependent origination; and (3) that it is also *anitya,* or impermanence. In addition to having a feeling for the organism and for matrices, a biocentric spirituality can and should have a feeling for suchness, dependent origination, and impermanence.

Emptiness as Suchness

As Masao Abe explains, suchness is the as-it-is-ness of an entity, the sheer occurrence of an entity as uncategorized, spontaneous happening in its own right. The suchness of an entity is the very realization of its spontaneity, its self-creativity, its moment-by-moment freedom:

> Suchness is not a static or fixed state but a dynamic and living basis from which the individual, and everything else in mutual interpenetration, begins its activity anew at every moment of the process. This is the activity of self-determination (freedom) based on the realization of Sunyata (Emptiness).

The realization of our own suchness and the prereflective awareness of the suchness of other beings is "the positive aspect of the realization of Emptiness."

> When you realize your own suchness, you realize the suchness of everything at once. A pine tree appears in its suchness. Bamboo manifests itself in its suchness. Dogs and cats appear in their suchness as well. A dog is really a dog. No more, no less. A cat is really a cat. No more, no less. Everything is realized in its distinctiveness.

This suchness "is not a goal to be reached." We "are never separated from suchness even for a moment." It is "the real point of departure for our lives and for our activity" (Abe 1985, 226).

The awareness of the suchness of other beings—of dogs and cats—can be an important feature of a biocentric spirituality. In *Zen and Japanese Culture*, D. T. Suzuki gives us a feeling for what this awareness can be like. Suzuki tells us that from a Zen perspective "we may treat Nature not as an object to conquer and turn wantonly to human service, but as a friend, as a fellow being, who is destined like ourselves for Buddhahood." Zen Buddhists "want us to meet Nature as a friendly, well-meaning agent whose inner being is thor-

oughly like our own" (1973, 351). To make his point Suzuki contrasts what he takes to be a typical Western, Christian approach to nature, as expressed by the English poet Tennyson, with a Zen approach as expressed by the Japanese master of haiku, Bashō.

The relevant lines from Tennyson's "Flower in the Crannied Wall" are as follows:

> Flower in the crannied wall,
> I pluck you out of the crannies,
> I hold you here, root and all, in my hand,
> Little flower—but *if* I could understand
> What you are, root and all, and all in all,
> I should know what God and man is.

Suzuki comments that Tennyson's approach is quite inquisitive and philosophical. The English poet seems to approach the flower as an abstraction, an object of intellectual scrutiny, a problem to be solved rather than an actuality to be accepted on its own terms. The inner spirit of his approach is exemplified by the fact that he chose to "pluck" it "root and all" instead of allowing it to grow of its own accord and on its own terms.

By contrast, says Suzuki, Bashō "was no scientist bent on analysis, nor was he a philosopher." Rather he was a poetic appreciator of the suchness of things. Walking along a road, he was awakened by something white by the roadside. It was a white flowering herb called a *nazuna* or, in English, a shepherd's purse. "The discovery must have called up a variety of feelings," Suzuki tells us, but the poet is not explicit about them. He simply writes:

> When closely inspected,
> The nazuna is flowering
> By the hedge.

As Suzuki puts it, the poet leaves "the pleasure of discovery and appreciation to the reader" (1973, 263).

And what is the reader to discover and appreciate? According to Suzuki, this poem and others are intended to disclose the suchness of the things: in this case the suchness—the as-it-is-ness—of the humble nazuna "with all its individuality, growing among other vegetation" (1973, 264). Here there is nothing symbolic about nature in general or the nazuna in particular. The nazuna does not point beyond itself to other objects: physical or mental, human or divine. It does not point to God as its Creator or to us as its beholders. Rather, the flower is simply itself, and noteworthy for that very reason.

To see something—say, a nazuna plant—in its suchness is to be aware of it as something that eludes complete categorization. In its

concrete appearance, the white presence that shows itself before our perceptual field and that we name "nazuna plant" is not completely captured by the word "nazuna" or by the concepts that accompany the word in our mind. There is something transconceptual and extralinguistic about the presence, something given in a nonverbal, strictly perceptual and intuitive way, that eludes categorization and yet makes it possible. This something is by no means an abstract property among properties; it is not something that adheres to the plant much as a coat of paint adheres to a billiard ball. Rather, it is the plant itself, as a dynamic happening, a creative expression of its own essence, Emptiness.

It is tempting to equate suchness with what in earlier chapters we called intrinsic value. Suchness, we might say, is the value an entity has for itself and in itself. Such an identification would, I think, be wrong.

Consider the fact that there can be degrees of intrinsic value. We know this not only by speculative though necessary comparisons between cancer cells and porpoises but also by introspection. At some times—in moments of despair, for example—we can have less value to ourselves than at others; and some moments of our experience—moments of lethargy or apathy, for example—can be less rich, or less desirable, than others. From introspection we know that sometimes our lives have less quality—less richness of experience and self-significance—than others. This quality is intrinsic value. Every time we seek richer experience, and every time we attempt to move beyond despair in our own lives, we implicitly acknowledge that intrinsic value occurs in degrees.

Suchness, however, does not. There is as much suchness in a moment of phlegmatic torpor as there is in one of vital awareness; as much as-it-is-ness in the pain suffered by a child in the Holocaust as there is in the joy felt by a father holding his firstborn; as much Emptiness in the sentience of a bacterium as in that of a dolphin. It is better, I believe, to define suchness as the *isness* or creativity of an entity, and then to define intrinsic value as the *quality* of that isness or creativity. Suchness names the existential fact that an entity actualizes itself in a certain way; intrinsic value names the subjective tone—the degree of harmony and intensity—that forms the content of that self-actualization. Intrinsic value and suchness always occur together, but they are two sides of a single coin.

If, as proposed, a feeling for the organism is a sensitivity to its intrinsic value, then the "intuition of suchness" is different from "feeling for the organism." When we have a feeling for the organism—another mammal, for example—we imagine ourselves inside the subjectivity of that organism, feeling its feelings. Usually some sort of judgment is involved, for we take on the interests of the organism at issue. If the organism has an interest in avoiding pain, and it seems to be experiencing pain, we judge the subjective situation of the organism to be "bad" or "undesirable." The intuition of suchness, on the other hand, is less emotional. It is simply a taking note of an entity as it appears, allowing the entity to show itself, without passing judgment. The intuition of suchness is itself more objective, and less projective, than a feeling for the organism. It is more like "being aware of an organism" than it is like "empathy for an organism." Nevertheless, the two can occur alternately or simultaneously. The intuition of suchness can support a feeling for the organism in at least two ways.

First, as Suzuki shows, it can help us to affirm that we share a common identity with all other actualities, regardless of whatever differences there might be in intrinsic value. All creatures are, after all, actualities among actualities: that is, instances of suchness. In Suzuki's words, inasmuch as other beings exemplify suchness, they have an inner being that is "thoroughly like our own." To be aware of the suchness of all things can be to recognize their commonality with us, and ours with them, and thus to feel united with them.

Second, the intuition of suchness can help us to recognize that our own categories of thought are limited, that there is something about beings in nature—humans included—that cannot be framed in words and names. To see things in their Emptiness is not only to appreciate the fact that we share a common essence; it is also to appreciate them in their extralinguistic otherness. If the empathy involved in a feeling for the organism is not to be overly sentimental and projective, it must be imbued with this respect for otherness. The intuition of suchness is part of such respect.

One organism, the suchness of whom Christians can learn to intuit, is God. To intuit the suchness of God is to allow God to be on God's own terms, to let God be God. Of course, God as thus understood is not a cosmic monarch, an autocratic ruler to whose arbitrary will human beings are obliged to conform. Nor is God an organism standing over and against other organisms. Rather, as suggested in the first chapter, God is that ultimate Life, that cosmic Heart, whose very body is the universe itself. To intuit the suchness of God is to feel the suchness of One of whose life we are a part and in whose life we live, move, and have our being. In the mode of suchness, God can be experienced as a personal presence: as a Mother, Lover, or Friend. But God can also be experienced as an imageless reality, a feeling discovered in silent, wordless prayer. Amid such prayer we can feel the sheer givenness of an embracing love that includes us within its scope, that wells up within us if we are open, and that extends outward to include the whole creation. This is a love we do not earn or create, yet nevertheless it lies at the center of our existence and that of everything else. To intuit the suchness of God in this way is to understand that the adventure of the universe as One is closely united with our own deepest self, that God is the very Heart of our hearts.

Emptiness as Pratitya-Samutpada

There is, however, more to Emptiness than suchness, at least as suchness has been described here. The language of self-actualization can suggest, wrongly, that a given entity—a nazuna, for example—has a self-enclosed "self" that then "actualizes itself" in isolation from the rest of the world. This is not the case. As Suzuki explains, the nazuna is interfused with every other actuality in the universe, including the poet Bashō. To say that things express Emptiness is to say that they arise and perish in a way that is utterly "empty" of self-enclosed autonomy and utterly "full" of dependence on others. To understand the Emptiness of an entity is to see it as an instance of what Buddhists call *pratitya-samutpada,* or dependent origination.

In order to understand dependent origination, the word "dependence" itself must be considered. Dependence can be understood in one or both of two ways. On the one hand, dependence can mean external influence. In this instance one entity "depends" on others because it is causally influenced by others. A living cell in the body of a nazuna plant depends on other cells inasmuch as its survival depends on receiving chemical and electrical influences from other cells. But dependence can also mean internal immanence. One entity can depend on others because the latter are actually immanent within, and thus constitutive of, the former. For example, a living cell in the body of a nazuna plant depends on the organelles that compose it because the latter are actually immanent within, and hence part of the very constitution of, the cell. They influence the cell from the inside rather than the outside.

In a Buddhist context, dependence can be understood in either or both of these two senses. To say that things are dependently originating can mean (1) that things are invariably influenced, or caused, by external conditions, and it can also mean (2) that things are invariably constituted by other things that are immanent within them. When Buddhists such as D. T. Suzuki speak of the interpenetration or interfusion of entities one with the other, they have in mind this second sense, mutual immanence. It is not just that a nazuna plant is influenced by things outside it, it is that the things outside it are also, in some way, within it. It depends on them because they are constitutive of it. Entities are really present in one another.

The closest analogy we have to this phenomenon is our own

experience, our own sentient awareness. When I am aware of something external to my body—say, a nazuna plant—the object of my
awareness, the plant, is within my experience. It is the objective
content of my subjective awareness. If I further recognize, as Zen
Buddhists recommend, that "I" myself am identical with my experience, then the nazuna plant is part of my very "I." My own self or
mind is constituted by the plant, plus whatever else I am aware of,
which is to say that the plant, or at least some aspect of it, is present
within me even as it is external to my body.

This is not solipsism. The fact that the plant is immanent within
me does not mean that I create it, or that it is a mere projection of
my ego, though surely I am creative and partly projective in the way
I interpret and understand it. Rather, it means that my experience
is itself a field of awareness with horizons that extend out beyond my
body to include the very world of which I am a part. As a sentient
being, I am within the world and the world is within me. In the
well-known phrase of Heidegger, my own existence is an act of
being-in-the-world.

A study of Zen and other forms of Buddhism suggests that all
beings are, in their own ways, acts of being-in-the-world. In each and
every individual entity, so the Buddhist claims through the doctrine
of *pratitya-samutpada,* the entire universe is enfolded as part of the
entity's very constitution. In the context of process theology, this
means all actual individuals—be they energy events in the depths of
an atom, living cells in a nazuna plant, psychosomatic organisms
such as pelicans and humans, or the divine Matrix who is God—are
organisms. This is to say that while they are individuals, they are not
self-enclosed or self-subsistent individuals. Rather they are—like
living cells composed of organelles—dependently originating, compound individuals. Compound individuals are not cut off from others
by the boundaries of their skins or membranes. Rather, they are
composed of, and constituted by, other beings.

Given this understanding of dependent origination as the immanence of entities in one another, freedom takes on a new light.
Freedom lies not in escaping the immanence of other entities within
one's own constitution but, rather, in integrating that immanence.
Organisms actualize themselves as self-actualizing wholes that creatively synthesize, moment by moment, the very parts of which they
are composed. That humans and other organisms dependently originate is an undeniable fact. *How* they do so is, at least in part, the
result of their freedom.

To be Empty, then, is to be fully relational and thus formed by
other things, even as one is self-creative. The ultimate reality of an
entity—its Emptiness—is its freedom *and* its dependent origination.

To be aware of an entity in its suchness is to be aware of it as a self-actualizing concrescence of the entire universe.

The recognition of compound individuality and of the immanence of the universe within each entity can further enrich a Christian biocentric spirituality. Just as the intuition of suchness provides an aid to having a "feeling for the organism," so the intuition of dependent origination provides an aid to a "feeling for matrices."

In the first place, it shows us that no individual whatsoever can exist apart from matrices. The world is utterly empty of atomized substances. This can help us to be sensitive to the fact that other beings are dependent on their surroundings and thus that we need to attend to their surroundings if we are to care for them. If children growing up in ghettoes are to enjoy life, ghettoes themselves must be replaced by hospitable habitats. And if endangered species are to survive, their habitats must be preserved. To care for living beings is to attend to the matrices in which they dependently originate and to recognize that, for good (in the case of endangered species) or ill (in the case of children in ghettoes), those matrices form part of their very being.

In the second place, the intuition of dependent origination can help us to recognize that we ourselves are compound individuals, that we ourselves dependently originate in relation to other beings, and that the natural world is immanent within us. We are not cut off from nature by our bodies; rather, our bodies are that aspect of nature with which, in life as we know it, we are most intimate. In truth, the whole world is our body. The American critic and essayist Joseph Wood Krutch expressed this intuition when he wrote, "Only those within whose consciousness the suns rise and set, the leaves burgeon and wither, can be said to be aware of what living is" (quoted in Tripp 1987, 426). The intuition of dependent origination can remind us that, in fact, the suns *do* rise and set, and the leaves *do* burgeon and wither within our consciousness, within our selves. Our task, as biocentric Christians and as human beings, is to recognize this fact, to identify with our surroundings, and then to live lightly on the Earth.

Four Horizons of Dependent Origination

The range of beings that dependently originate within us, and to which we may be open in a biocentric spirituality, is wide indeed. In a seminal essay called "Building Dwelling Thinking," Heidegger provides a helpful metaphor to understand this range. There he discusses *dwelling,* which he understands to be the essential way in which human beings exist, or at least can exist, in the world. He pays particular attention to the role of artifacts such as bridges and houses in authentic dwelling, and he sees such artifacts as a gathering together, or a bringing into relational presence, four horizons: earth and sky, divinities and mortals. The phrase "earth and sky, divinities and mortals" provides the metaphor we need.

Speaking of a small, rustic bridge that runs across a stream, Heidegger tries to illustrate his point. He tells us that "the bridge gathers to itself in its own way earth and sky, divinities and mortals." It brings the Earth into presence by being constructed of it and by providing a context for a landscape surrounding the waters. It brings the sky into presence by inviting us to attend, as we look at the bridge itself, to the space, extending into the heavens, beneath which it sits. It brings mortals into presence by being a place where they cross to get from "the castle to the cathedral square." And it brings the gods and goddesses into presence by being a place where spirits dwell, whether we know it or not.

> The bridge gathers, as a passage that crosses, before the divinities—whether we explicitly think of, and visibly give thanks for, their presence, as in the figure of the saint of the bridge, or whether that divine presence is obstructed or even pushed wholly aside (1977, 331).

Together Heidegger speaks of earth and sky, divinities and mortals as the "fourfold." His point is that the bridge makes room for the fourfold to disclose itself, that in its own way it both admits and installs the four horizons in terms of which we live.

It is unnecessary for our purposes to exposit further Heidegger's particular understanding of the fourfold. What is important is that he names the general horizons to which a Christian biocentric spirituality can be open in its appreciation of Emptiness as *pratitya-samutpada*. The Earth is what it is in relation to the sky, which is what it is in relation to the gods, who are what they are in relation to mortals, all of which are immanent within us as constitutive of our lives, even as they also have integrity in their own right.

For us the word "earth" can symbolize the planet on which we dwell, including the physical matter of which it and our own bodies are made. Earth can refer to the realm of the terrestrial and inorganic, including water and air as well as land. When we are in touch with the Earth, we see the beauty, strength, and fragility of the finite. We fittingly respond with an appreciation of physical matter, a love for the concrete, an awareness of finitude, and, as emphasized earlier, a feeling for matrices.

The word "sky" can symbolize the heavens beneath which we stand and, of late, into which we have sent satellites and probes. Sky can refer to the celestial and cosmic, including as it does a presently expanding cosmos, or, alternatively, to the Earth's atmosphere as such. When we are in touch with the sky, we sense the presence of the unbounded and unlimited: that which inspires our imaginations to explore possibilities for hope amid hopelessness. Through openness to the sky, we ourselves become more open to the divine lure, from which, indeed, new possibilities continually emerge. Appropriate spiritual responses to the sky include wonder, fantasy, and hope.

The word "divinities" can symbolize the spirits—be they gods or goddesses—that we sometimes discover within our own psyches: in dreams, for example. They are the Jungian archetypes and other entities of our subconscious. They include all subconscious entities that, not accessible to our senses, nevertheless have power in us, with us, and, at times, over us. When we are in touch with these spirits, we realize that there are dimensions and domains other than the three-dimensional space that we encounter with our eyes, and that in these other dimensions there may well dwell inhabitants in relation to which we exist. A biocentric spirituality can be open to divinities as revelations of a collective unconscious and, in some instances, as windows to the divine, revelations of diverse aspects of the divine mystery.

The word "mortals" can symbolize human beings, other animals, and plants. Mortals refers to those life forms that have taken centuries to evolve on our planet, and that are subject to death or, alternatively, to those particular life forms that suffer death in ways analogous to ourselves. When we are in touch with mortals, we sense the presence of other subjects with which we can exist in communion and care. Appropriate responses include a "feeling for the organism."

A biocentric spirituality can be open in different ways to each of these domains: to earth and sky, divinities and mortals. It can recognize that each are what they are in relation to the other and that all are expressions of Emptiness. It can further affirm that God, the cosmic Heart that in her own way is an all-inclusive expression of Emptiness, lures us to be open to the fourfold relative to our own circumstances and needs and to the circumstances and needs of others. Indeed, it can say that God is potentially disclosed through each and all of the four domains and that God yearns to redeem sentient beings in each of the domains. God herself is not a domain among domains but, rather, the cosmic life in whom all domains dwell, even as they also dwell in our conscious and subconscious experience.

Emptiness as Impermanence

Earth and sky, divinities and mortals are by no means static. In relation to one another, they form a dance of sorts, for within and apart from our own consciousness they are forever in motion, perpetually changing and perpetually perishing. The divine Lover, too, is a dancer: adapting her life-enriching aims and intentions to the movements of the world, sometimes leading and sometimes responding, always caring. The fluidity of the world, as one expression of Emptiness, is forever accompanied by the fluidity of God, as another.

As Christians move toward a biocentric spirituality, it is important that we acquire a feeling for this fluidity, or, as Buddhists put it, this *anitya,* which is best translated "impermanence." Indeed, impermanence is the third aspect of Emptiness—in addition to suchness and dependent origination—from which Christians can learn.

Among the things we can learn—a lesson that is a reminder of truths already known in the Bible—is the fact that we ourselves are impermanent. This is the case, not only in the sense that we will perish as biological organisms at the end of our lives, but in the sense that we—as individual streams of experience extending from birth (and perhaps before) to death (and perhaps beyond)—are dying at each moment. As Masao Abe explains in discussing the traditional Buddhist doctrine of transmigration, "If we grasp the process of transmigration, not from the outside . . . but from within . . . then we are always living and always dying at every moment" (1985, 165). Death in its deepest sense is not something that occurs only at the end of our lives, it is something that occurs every time the immediacy of a momentary experience in our life stream perishes. For we, as living persons, are identical with this life stream and its experiences. As the immediacy of an experience perishes, so, at that moment, do we.

To say that we die at each moment is not to deny a continuity of personal experiences over time, or the possibility of continuity beyond this life. In life as we know it, as one experience in the life stream perishes, another succeeds it. In this sense, we not only die at every moment, we are reborn at every moment. Continuity is established through the actual influence of prior experiences on successive experiences as effected through subconscious and conscious memory. As argued in chapter 1, it is possible that rebirth of this sort occurs beyond physical death, such that, for humans and nonhumans, certain forms of redemption occur. This is a profound and important Christian hope.

To say that we die at each moment is to say, however, that there is a discontinuity amid the continuity (Abe 1985, 166). Even if we and other creatures are renewed after physical death, we will be dying at each moment then, just as we are doing so now. We are not just one self, we are many selves, and each self lives only for a moment, be it in this life or the next. Masao Abe and other members of the Kyoto School of Japanese philosophy insist on the importance of fully internalizing this death dimension of life and thus of coming to grips with the inescapability of impermanence. As the ultimate reality, they say, Emptiness is not a timeless absolute in which to rest; it is the very impermanence of each and every moment of existence. Stated another way, it is dependent cessation as well as dependent origination. Abe insists that this truth applies not only to humans but to every finite existent. It ought also to apply, so he insists, in a friendly but serious admonition to Christians, to God.

In Buddhism, the primary reason why it is important to recognize impermanence is that this recognition facilitates a release from the illusion of permanence and the suffering that ensues from it. According to Buddhists, humans often seek, wrongly and to their own detriment, two kinds of nonexistent objects: self-existent objects that depend on nothing except themselves for their existence and permanent objects that are utterly changeless. Often these nonexistent objects are collapsed into a single imagined reality, a permanent substance of one sort or another. God has sometimes been conceived as such a substance, as has the human self. Given this way of thinking about God or the self, the search for God and self will always be frustrated. There is no changeless God, and there is no changeless self.

Not only do *we* suffer in the search for nonexistent substances, so do others at our expense. For sometimes we approach other sentient beings as if they were permanent substances, and when we approach them this way they often become for us objects to be owned rather than subjects to be appreciated. If we are parents, we can approach our children this way, not allowing them to change; if we are wives or husbands, we can approach our spouses this way, not allowing them to grow; if we are employers, we can approach employees this way, not allowing them to develop their own potential in surprising ways. In each case we approach living subjects with intrinsic value as if they were mere objects. We neglect the fact that other people exist—as do we ourselves—from moment to moment, and that while each moment of a life can have its harmony and intensity, no moment can be owned as a permanent possession, either by the person living it or by others.

Christians developing a biocentric spirituality have much to learn from this Buddhist emphasis on impermanence. In the first place, we can learn to appreciate the transience, and hence the potential or actual beauty, of each moment in our lives and in the lives of other creatures. We can learn to measure the quality of our lives and that of others in units both smaller and closer to lived experience than those to which we are accustomed. This is to appreciate the fact, as

Elie Wiesel puts it in describing the time frame of the prophet Jeremiah, that life "is made of minutes, not necessarily years, and surely not centuries" (1981, 121).

Furthermore, for some creatures life is made of seconds and microseconds. God loves each creature, and us as well, in terms of the concrete, impermanent moments that constitute our lives. A biocentric spirituality will be sensitive to this fact, learning to see and appreciate nonhuman creatures in time frames relative to those moments in terms of which they live.

In the second place, we can learn from the Buddhist emphasis on impermanence that God, too, is fluid and hence not to be clung to. As an expression of Emptiness, the God in whom we place our trust, and through whose grace we hope for redemption, both for ourselves and for all other sentient beings, is herself impermanent in at least two senses.

First, like a creative bodhisattva, she adapts to each situation. This means among other things that the content of her lure changes with changing situations. In human life, for example, sometimes we are called to modify circumstances in which we find ourselves, fighting to live amid the threat of death, and sometimes we are called to accept the circumstances in which we find ourselves, accepting death as an inevitability and perhaps even a friend. We cannot cling to God as she appears in the form of a lure because the content of her lure is itself changing.

To say that God adapts to each situation also means that the very content of her empathy—more particularly, the identity she assumes in order to meet the needs of creatures—changes with changing circumstances. Always God assumes the character that is most needed by the creature at issue, given its circumstances. For pelicans, God becomes, in her own heart, a pelican; for cockroaches, a cockroach; for cats, a cat; for earthworms, an earthworm; for humans, a human.

The fluidity of God has important implications for how we conceive her. As distinct from other animals, humans can respond to God's changing personality by imagining her in personal terms. While the pelican may not imagine God as a pelican, we can imagine God as somehow analogous to a human personality. The fluidity of God allows us to say that God becomes the kind of person that is most needed by the person at issue in order for that person to find wholeness and help others to become whole. She becomes a father for those who need a father, a lover for those who need a lover, a friend for those who need a friend, a mother for those who need a mother. In a given person's life, the identity of God may itself change from moment to moment, relative to changing needs and circumstances. From the outside this can look like serial polytheism: moving from one god to another. From the inside, however, it is a variegated, flexible monotheism: approaching God through different faces she assumes. Amid her fluidity, God is always the same God, though flowing and changing like a river, rather than static and changeless like a rock. She is constant in her love, but her constancy is dynamic and adaptive. To have faith in her is not to hold on to her as the one exception to change. Rather, it is to trust in the flow of her grace, to trust that whatever situation we are in, she will be there as a companion working to guide us toward the fullness of life.

A second way in which God is impermanent concerns momentariness and the perishing of experiential immediacy. As has been said, Buddhists aver that the human self, and by implication the animal psyche, is best understood as a series of momentary experiences, and that the immediacy of a predecessor experience perishes in order to make way for successor experiences. It is possible that this way of thinking about the human psyche is also appropriate for thinking about the divine Psyche. It is possible that God, too, dies in the immediacy of each moment of her existence, then to be reborn at the next moment. Her existence would be beginningless and endless, yet living and dying at each moment.

The value of recognizing this way of thinking about God for a biocentric Christianity is not simply that it allows for greater consistency by making God an expression of, rather than an exception to, Emptiness. The value is that it encourages Christians to realize even more fully that the acceptance of impermanence is itself an aspect of that wholeness, that shalom, toward which we are called by God. For God's completeness, too, may lie in an acceptance of impermanence. God too may be awakened to the truth of Emptiness.

The idea that God knows perishing from the inside—that God, too, dies in some sense—is not necessarily unchristian. This "death of God" is implicit in the traditional Christian idea that God partook of Jesus' own death on the cross, that God knew then, and knows now, what it means to die. A biocentric Christianity can extend this insight to say, not simply that God knows what it means to die, but that God does indeed die from moment to moment. The cross can be a symbol, among other things, for this perpetual death that God undergoes.

On the other side of the cross, of course, is the resurrection. The biocentric Christian can trust that, after each death, there is in God a resurrection, a rebirth. He or she can recognize that the ultimate meaning of a finite life, human or nonhuman, lies in contributing to this divine resurrection, which itself follows every death. With God, so the Christian can hope, all sentient beings are resurrected, not in the sense that they escape impermanence but rather in the sense that they are remembered, in their concreteness, in the divine memory.

In God's moment-by-moment rebirth, awakened as it may be at each moment to the truth of impermanence, all moments of life on Earth are remembered with the tender care of a cosmic bodhisattva. Their momentary harmonies become part of the divine harmony; their momentary intensities contribute to the divine intensity. In this contribution to divine beauty—a beauty for which the eros of life aims at every moment—lies life's fulfillment.

4

A Postpatriarchal Christianity

On a cold November morning in South Texas when I was ten years old, I spotted a white-tailed buck in a forest of mesquite trees. He was in a clearing about thirty yards from where I sat in a hunter's stand with my father. Shaking from the cold, I stuck my gun out the window. With the barrel wavering back and forth in my unsteady hands, it was hard to get the neck of the deer in the sights of my rifle. But I knew I had to shoot. I didn't have to prove myself to my father; he would love me no matter what. But I had to prove myself to countless other men who had entered my ten-year-old consciousness. I had seen them in advertisements and at the movies. Some of them wore cowboy hats, rode in rodeos, drank beer, and knew how to keep women in their places; others wore dark suits, drove fine cars, drank whiskey, and were surrounded by adoring women in sequined dresses. All these men were in complete control of their emotions. They never cried, except on rare occasions when it was manly to do so, and then only briefly, without noise. I had to show these mythical, paradigmatic men that I was one of them. "Being a man" meant seeing the buck not as a creature loved for his own sake by God, much less by men, but as a mere object: a set of antlers to be hung on the wall in my room. It meant being able to kill the buck without being sentimental about it.

So despite the wavering of the barrel, I pulled the trigger. The gun fired, and I was briefly knocked back by its kick. In a split second I recovered and looked out the window to see what had happened. I saw the buck lying on his side, clawing the ground with his left front leg. I had hit him in the back; he was injured and in pain.

My father and I quickly got out of the stand and walked toward him. The buck's eyes had a terrified look in them, and I thought I heard a grunting sound coming from his mouth. Despite the self-imposed pressure not to show any emotion, I cried. My father gently told me that I needed to shoot him again. I wasn't sure why, but I knew my father was right, so I got about ten feet from him, put the rifle to my shoulder, and again took aim. With my arms still shaking, this time from being so upset by the sight of the deer clawing at the ground, I missed. I tried again, and missed again. I must have shot and missed five times. Finally I gave my gun to my father and asked him to kill the deer. With one shot it was over.

As we were nearing the deer to begin gutting him, I remember asking my father, "Dad, do deer *feel?*" In my own way, I was asking many of the questions raised in this book: Are other animals subjects in their own right? Do they have perspectives of their own? Do they experience pleasure and pain? Do they care about surviving? Do they have value in and for themselves? Do they have rights that we ought to respect? Does God care about them?

I don't remember what my father told me, but it didn't really matter. Deep down I knew the answer to my question even before my father could respond. I had sense enough to know that when a buck claws at the ground and has a look of terror in his eyes, he is in pain. I knew that I had harmed a kindred creature, not for the meat I could acquire from his body, though we did in fact eat him. I harmed this deer for the manhood I could gain from killing him.

I do not tell this story to condemn all hunting. Those who aspire to a life-centered Christianity can recognize that hunting has played, and in some parts of the world continues to play, a valuable yet also ambiguous role in human survival. Particularly when hunters kill with a reverence for the animals whose lives they take, when they do so in order to obtain food, and when food cannot be obtained in any other way, hunting is a much more honorable way to gain sustenance than is the buying of meat at a local supermarket. Hunters can take responsibility for the fact that they have taken a life; they can kill with reverence. When we buy meat at supermarkets, we are usually oblivious to the fact that our neatly packaged purchase was once a kindred creature, and that, if "produced" in a factory farm, this creature, this subject of divine love, had almost no opportunities for quality existence.

In telling this story, however, I *do* mean to criticize the ideal of manhood in the name of which I shot the buck. A life-centered Christianity must oppose that image of masculinity which shaped my own imagination at age ten and no doubt continues to shape it today. It must resist that kind of "manhood," itself promulgated in so many world civilizations, which sees other living beings as mere means to human ends and fails to recognize that life, all of life, is precious to, and part of, the divine Life. The best way Christianity can evolve into a life-affirming religion is for Christians, women and men, to give up the twin ideas (1) that men must be stereotypically masculine, at least given the image of masculinity just described, and (2) that God is a sovereign, all-controlling expression of an exclusively masculine spirit.

To this end feminist theologies can help, for they have shown that there are deep historical connections between male-centeredness and human-centeredness, androcentrism and anthropocentrism. What has motivated men to keep women in their place or to surround themselves with adoring women has also motivated many of us to keep other animals in their place and to be surrounded by a subservient Earth. It is no accident, so feminists would suggest, that my own image of the "manly man" at age ten was one who could approach other animals and women as objects for self-aggrandizement rather than as ends in themselves. The very way of thinking that objectifies women into mere objects of male desire has also objectified the Earth and other living beings into objects of human use.

This way of thinking has seeped into much historical Christianity. In certain respects it has been a part of Christian consciousness since biblical times. Those who hope for a new, life-centered consciousness among Christians rightly hope for a radical evolution within Christianity: the emergence of a new, postpatriarchal Christianity. In previous chapters I have described a panentheistic understanding of God (chapter 1), an ethical perspective that respects both life and environment (chapter 2), and an empathic and relational style of spirituality (chapter 3), all of which I have endorsed as "life-centered." If these ideas are to be adopted by large numbers of Christians in the foreseeable future, if the ideas are to find ecclesial homes, it will most likely be in the form of a new postpatriarchal Christianity.

Not only is it probable that biocentric ideas will become part of Christianity only inasmuch as Christianity becomes postpatriarchal, it is desirable that this be the case. For feminist theologies, more than other emancipatory perspectives, unite the two concerns that a life-centered orientation must involve: a concern for the Earth and its nonhuman creatures plus a concern for people. Influenced by the trailblazing work of Rosemary Radford Ruether (1975) and Elizabeth Dodson Gray (1979), both of whom showed links between the oppression of women and that of nature, feminist theologies generally recognize that these two concerns are inseparable and that the very theme of liberation, so central to Christianity as it evolves into a new century, must extend both to marginalized people and to other living beings. Lest a biocentric Christianity neglect people in its extension of liberation to the nonhuman world, it must drink deeply from the wells of feminist thought. It must be part of a broader movement toward a postpatriarchal Christianity.

To whatever degree it is realized, this Christianity will be freeing for women. It will enable women to discover and create their own identities as women. But it will also be freeing for men, liberating us from images of masculinity that deny us opportunities for our own full humanity. In order for the transition to occur, new leadership is needed within existing churches, which heretofore have been controlled primarily by men. Most of this leadership must be female. Fortunately this new leadership is emerging. Feminist theologies represent part of its leading edge.

Of course, as many women clergy within Christian churches can attest, the emergence of a postpatriarchal Christianity will not be easy. For at least four thousand years the creeds, codes, and cults of the world's most populous religions have been controlled by men in power. Men, not women, have been the primary social and imaginative engineers of Judaism, Christianity, Islam, Hinduism, Buddhism, Taoism, Confucianism, and Shintoism. Consider, for example, a list of those prime religious movers upon whom introductions to the world religions so often focus: Abraham, Moses, Jesus, and Muhammad in the West; Gautama, Mahavira, Shankara, and Ramanuja in India; Confucius, Mencius, Lao-tzu, and Chuang-tzu in China; and Shinran, Honen, Dōgen, and Nichiren in Japan. Of course, women too have been involved in the development of the world religions. But they have not been equal partners. More often than not, they have worked in homes and behind the scenes to help men in positions of leadership; and all too often—as the histories of European witch burning, Indian widow burning, and Chinese foot-binding attest—they have been victims of male-defined religious ideologies. Mary Daly does not exaggerate in saying that for at least four thousand years patriarchy has been, and still is, "the prevailing religion of the entire planet." As she puts it, "All of the so-called religions legitimating patriarchy are mere sects subsumed under its vast umbrella/canopy" (Daly 1978, 39).

For most feminist philosophers and theologians, the word "patriarchy" has two meanings. It refers to a social system in which men rule women economically, politically, and culturally. And it refers to a way of thinking and feeling, guided by a conceptual framework, that supports and legitimates this social system. This way of thinking and feeling can be internalized by women as well as men, and it may or may not be a subject of conscious reflection. As philosopher Karen Warren explains, "Whether we know it or not, each of us operates out of a socially constructed mind set or conceptual framework, i.e., a set of beliefs, values, attitudes, and assumptions which shape, reflect, and explain our view of ourselves and our world" (1987, 6). When I use the word "patriarchy" in this chapter, I mean it primarily in the second sense.

The particular ideas and images within a patriarchal conceptual framework need not be about women in order to affect women.

Instead they may deal with the nature of the human self, or the good life, or the world as a whole, or God. When in the West, for example, Christians have imaged God as male, that very imagery, though apparently referring to the divine rather than the human, has nevertheless suggested to many men, and to women as well, that women are less godlike than men, and hence that women are rightly subjugated to men. And when the good life has been imaged as one that is in complete control of nonhuman nature, that very image, though apparently referring only to nature, has nevertheless led to the view that women, too, are to be controlled or tamed because they have been symbolically identified with nature.

Furthermore, as Ruether has persuasively shown (1975, 14), it is not exclusively women who have been detrimentally affected by patriarchy. At least in the West, images that have supported male rule over women have also supported the rule of rich over poor, race over race, culture over culture, and humanity over nature. The attitudes that have enabled sexism to persist also enable classism, racism, cultural chauvinism, and anthropocentrism to persist. As the work of Warren suggests, this is because Western patriarchal thinking has been characterized by three features: value-hierarchical thinking, a logic of domination, and certain conceptual dualisms.

Value-hierarchical thinking is thinking that consciously or subconsciously tends to categorize differences—for example, between men and women, or rich and poor, or light skin and dark skin, or humanity and nature—in terms of the spatial metaphor of "up" versus "down," evaluating one group as "higher" than, and thus superior to, the other. Warren does not argue that evaluations of superior and inferior are inevitably illegitimate. Indeed, she deems a nonsexist society superior to a sexist one. Rather, she proposes that Western patriarchal thinking has been prone to draw hierarchical distinctions *at the expense* of recognizing and appreciating valuable forms of diversity. Western patriarchal thinking has been prone to rank differences at the expense of appreciating them. Amid this tendency, women and others have been seen and treated as inferior. They have been viewed not only as different from the men in power but as inferior to them.

A logic of domination is a logic that issues from value-hierarchical thinking and that "explains, justifies, and maintains the subordination of an 'inferior' group by a 'superior' group on the grounds of the alleged inferiority or superiority of the respective group" (1987, 6). In the process it justifies the right of one group to exercise unilateral power over the other. From the perspective of the one exercising unilateral power, the power may itself be for good or ill. In either case it is power over rather than power with. In the West this is the power that God has been said to have in relation to the world: the power to influence without being influenced, the power to shape without being shaped. It is also the power, so Warren claims, that many men in the West have thought they ought to exercise over women and nature, people of color, and the poor.

Conceptual dualisms are dichotomized items of reflection—such as the human and the nonhuman, the mind and the body, the self and the other, history and nature, reason and emotion—in which the items themselves are conceived as essentially independent and mutually exclusive. To think in terms of dualisms is to think in terms of mutually external substances, or self-enclosed atoms, and it is to think in terms of either/or rather than both/and. It is to believe, for example, that reason and feeling are essentially independent of each other and that one must either be rational or emotional, not both; or that the self and the world are mutually external and that one must either love the self or love the world, not both. Oftentimes, so Warren suggests, hierarchical thinking has been applied to conceptual dualisms, so that one side of the dualism is valued "up" and the other "down." Warren avers that women and others have often been associated with items on the "down" side: with feeling rather than reason, with body rather than mind, with nature rather than history. In the process they have been subjugated to the "higher" powers: the men associated with mind, reason, and history.

To criticize patriarchy is not to suggest that patriarchal social systems have been bereft of created goods. In the West alone, witness the music of Bach, Mozart, and Beethoven; the literature of Chaucer, Dante, and Shakespeare; the painting of Michelangelo, Rembrandt, and Picasso; the philosophy of Plato, Aristotle, and Marx; and the science of Newton, Darwin, and Einstein. These goods emerged out of, and with the support of, patriarchal social arrangements. Consider also the countless lives of unnamed men and women from all walks of life who have lived and died with satisfaction amid patriarchal social arrangements, and who have found meaning in patriarchy. It would itself be simpleminded—and patriarchal—to draw a sharp dualism between patriarchy and postpatriarchy and then to treat one as unambiguously good compared to the other as unambiguously evil. Patriarchy is not the root of all evil, and all evil will not be eliminated in an elimination of patriarchy. Any given social system and way of thinking has involved, and will involve, both good and evil.

To criticize patriarchy is to recognize, however, that opportunities for cultural achievement in patriarchal social systems have not been equally shared, and that social benefits have been won at a great cost—in lives and in well-being—to *many* women, *many* poor, *many* people of color, *many* nonhuman animals, and *much* land. For the victims of patriarchal social arrangements, the benefits and achievements have not outweighed the costs. Feminists rightly hope for something better in the future. They call for the envisioning of alternative, postpatriarchal perspectives that can help guide us—women and men alike—beyond an age of male rule and its attendant oppressions toward an age of greater peace, justice, and ecological sustainability: that is, an age in which a biocentric ethic can itself flourish.

It is with the envisioning of such alternative perspectives, aligned with hope for alternative futures, that theology enters. For the task of theology—at least of Christian theology influenced by prophetic biblical traditions—is not simply to interpret inherited symbols of thought; it is to imagine new and hopeful ways of thinking and feeling in light of existing needs in the present. This is to exercise what biblical scholar Walter Brueggemann calls "the prophetic imagination," the task of which is "to nurture, nourish, and evoke a consciousness and perception alternative to the consciousness and perception of the dominant culture around us" (1978, 13). Of course, in the latter decades of the twentieth century, Christian theology has very little influence in secular colleges and universities around the world. When theologians speak, few academicians listen. But some forms of Christian theology do have considerable influence outside secular colleges and universities. They influence faculties in seminaries, who in turn influence church leaders, who in turn influence practicing religious communities. Religious communities are formidable influences in the world today. Christians alone number almost a quarter of the world's population. In this way one of the least prestigious of intellectual endeavors in the academy is one of the most influential in the world. And for this reason it is immensely important that theology seek to become postpatriarchal. In Christianity the possibility of a full-fledged postpatriarchal theology will for a long time remain an ideal rather than a reality. But it is an ideal worth striving toward and being striven toward. Even today some theological perspectives come closer than others to approximating it.

What ideas might constitute contemporary approximations of a postpatriarchal vision? And what role do women have, on the one hand, and men, on the other, in shaping these ideas? The purpose of the remainder of this chapter is to suggest answers to these questions. In the first of the chapter's three sections, I provide an introduction to Christian feminist theology for the general reader, in which I discuss the role of women and men in the development of postpatriarchal perspectives. This section is written for those readers who are interested in gender bias in society but who are not acquainted with contemporary attempts to overcome such biases in contemporary theology. The next two sections of the chapter are written for the specialist and nonspecialist alike. In the second section I show how the very theology I used in the previous chapters to develop a life-centered understanding of God, ethics, and spirituality—namely, process theology—can also be used by women and men alike to create postpatriarchal religious perspectives. In the third section I illustrate the outcome of such joint theologizing by identifying, discussing, and endorsing six characteristics of a process postpatriarchal Christianity.

I. Women, Men, and Postpatriarchal Theology

I have suggested that patriarchal thinking in the West involves value-hierarchical thinking, a logic of dominance, and certain conceptual dualisms. These three traits are not necessarily characteristic of patriarchal thinking throughout the world. A Buddhist culture, for example, might involve a patriarchal way of thinking that emphasizes interconnectedness and relationality rather than atomized dualisms. The point to make is that a patriarchal way of thinking, whatever its content, is one that functions to legitimate and support male rule.

Androcentrism as a Universal Characteristic of Patriarchy

However, despite the possibility of global variation in the content of patriarchal thinking, one aspect of such thinking seems universal. Patriarchal conceptual frameworks are almost always male-centered, or androcentric, in two interrelated ways. First, they repress and devalue women and women's experience as an authentic source of insight and vision for both women and men. Second, they universalize and absolutize male experience as representative of human experience in general. These two aspects of androcentrism constitute the "gender bias" that has so often been characteristic of the world's most populous religions.

The devaluation of women and women's experience in Western religious thought has been well documented, ranging from Paul's injunctions that women should remain silent in church because they can ask their husbands questions at home (1 Cor. 14:34–35), through Aquinas' view (following Aristotle) that women are "misbegotten males," to Ignatius of Loyola's view that Satan conducts himself "like a woman" in that he is weak before a show of strength but a tyrant if he has his will. Such devaluation is also characteristic of Eastern religions. In Confucianism, for example, a woman's role was to serve her parents, her husband, and her husband's parents, producing along the way sons for her husband. And the Buddha had to be persuaded, against his own inclinations to the contrary, to allow the creation of an order of nuns: an order on which he laid eight special regulations and which he strictly subordinated to the order of monks. For Gautama and Confucius as for Paul and Ignatius, the experiences of women as women did not rank equally with that of men.

The second characteristic of androcentric ways of thinking—the universalizing and absolutizing of male experience—has been part of the very method of much global theology and philosophy. In his description of his own method of philosophizing, Thomas Hobbes, the Western philosopher, captures the nature of androcentric method. Hobbes writes that "from the similitude of the thoughts and passions of one man to the thoughts and passions of another, whosoever looketh into himself, and considereth what he doth when he does think, opine, reason, hope, fear, etc. . . . he shall thereby read and know what are the thoughts and passions of all other men upon like occasions" (quoted in Zimmerman 1987, 21). It does not seem to have occurred to Hobbes that his own experience might be shaped by his gender, and that his experience might not represent the experience of women.

The result of such one-sided universalizing is that norms are established that, though imposed on and internalized by women, are not necessarily relevant to women, or even to other men. Consider one example. In Western theology, which until recent times has been almost completely created by men, sin has often been identified with pride and virtue with self-sacrificial love. The men who have proclaimed this—Reinhold Niebuhr and Paul Tillich, to give two examples from the twentieth century—have generally believed that their claims were relevant to all humans under any circumstances. Drawing from studies of women's experience, theologians such as Valerie Saiving (1979), Sue Dunfee (1982), and Judith Plaskow (1980) point out the limitations of such universalizations. They show that the gospel of self-sacrificial love may be quite relevant to men who enjoy a healthy degree of positive self-regard and have strong egos to be sacrificed, but that it is much less relevant, and sometimes destructive, to those women and powerless men who suffer from negative self-regard and who need, if not an ego to be sacrificed, then at least a self to be possessed. For them a one-sided emphasis on the virtues of self-sacrificial love leads wrongly to an underdevelopment or negation of self. In the Christian tradition, had women been co-creators of theology, such androcentric one-sidedness might have been avoided.

Feminist Theologies and Postpatriarchal Theologies

But why, after all, has androcentrism prevailed in so many of the world religions? The underlying reasons are complex. From different ends of the political spectrum, proposed explanations include cultural conditioning, male conspiracy, female complicity, biological determination, or various combinations thereof. Here we need not speculate on the reasons. Whatever the reasons, one thing is clear. Slowly but surely, among creative minorities in some quarters of the religious world, things are changing.

This is particularly though not exclusively the case in Protestant Christianity in the West. Beginning with movements one hundred years ago related to public education, women began to study Hebrew, Greek, and Latin along with men, which then enabled them to read the Bible in the original and ancient languages and, in the words of Constance Parvey, "uncover some of the interpretive biases that men interpreters and translators had imposed on scripture" (1984, 176).

Within the past twenty-five years, the pace has quickened considerably. Women have gained increasing access to seminaries, pulpits, and theological faculties. In just eight years, between 1976 and 1986, the number of women enrolled in Masters of Divinity programs in mainline Protestant denominations in the United States increased 200 percent, compared to a 9.6 percent increase among men. In some of these seminaries women now constitute from one-third to one-half of the total enrollment (cf. Wheeler 1981, 382). These seminarians are themselves influenced and enriched by feminist theologies of a variety of types: Christian and Jewish, post-Christian and post-Jewish, First World and (to a lesser extent) Third World, white and (to a lesser extent) black. Indeed, feminist theologies are among the most original and promising of religious visions now available, though the fact that they have been developed primarily by white women in the First World means that in future they need to be supplemented and criticized by complementary visions developed by women of color. This is already occurring among black women with "womanist" perspectives and among Third World women (cf. Russell et al.).

Feminist theologies often have two aims. First, they are *critical,* which means that they attempt to unmask the gender biases of classical theologies. Second, they are *constructive,* which means that they attempt to create new understandings of self, world, and the divine. These new understandings are intended to speak to the experiences of women in ways that patriarchal religious perspectives have not. To speak *to* the experience of women is both to illuminate where women have been under patriarchy and to show where they can be after patriarchy. In terms of world religions, such "speaking" is historically unique. Most male-designed theologies have spoken about and for women, but they have not spoken to women in terms women themselves have defined.

In many instances, to speak to the experience of women is to speak *about* the experience of men. Many feminist theologies do this by attempting to understand how and why men have been responsible for, and influenced by, patriarchy. They describe male behavior, and in so doing they imagine the inner intentions, attitudes, and dispositions of men. Such imaginative activity is indispensable for feminist theology. It would seem that, if male rule is to be overcome, it must be understood, and if it is to be understood, men themselves must be understood, though such understanding should not be the primary project of feminist theology. The primary project is to create feminist visions; men are understood only with this end in mind. Of course, generalizations concerning men are dangerous, because men, like women, are different within given societies, and from one society to another, and from one individual to another. Feminist theologians, for example, readily acknowledge that "feminist theology" itself has been for the most part a white woman's movement, subject to the racial limitations of being white. But generalizations are also inevitable and important. Without them, there is no insight.

Sometimes, as is the case with Ruether's thought, feminist theologies also attempt to speak *to* the experience of men. Either explicitly or implicitly, they indicate postpatriarchal ways of thinking, feeling, and acting by which men's lives, too, might be informed. This too is an act of the imagination, and a hopeful act at that, because men also have been victimized by patriarchal machismo. By conforming to patriarchal images of "masculinity," men have been denied a realization of their own full humanity. They have been strong at the expense of being vulnerable, rational at the expense of being emotional, assertive at the expense of being receptive.

Given the originality and promise of feminist theologies for men as well as for women, it is understandable that men might want to join women in creating feminist theologies. Unfortunately, they— we—cannot. As the phrase has generally come to be used, "feminist theology" does not only mean theology that speaks *to* the experience of women and perhaps to men. It also means theology that speaks *from* the experience of women as women. Feminist theologies are theologies created—usually by women—out of women's experience as that experience has been partially shaped by, and partially transcends, patriarchy. These theologies may speak truths relevant to men, but they speak these truths as they emerge out of woman's experience. It is as difficult for a man to do feminist theology as it is for a North American to do Latin American liberation theology, or for a white to do black theology.

What, then, can men do? It is important that men do something, for, barring an unforeseen shift in power relations throughout the world, it is doubtful that patriarchy itself can be overcome without some male cooperation. In the area of religion, I submit, men can do two things. First, and most important, we can internalize the critical insights of feminist theologies and attempt to rid our own visions and practices of gender bias. This takes time, patience, study, openness to change, receptivity to criticism, and a willingness to relinquish dominating power. Second, we can attempt to construct perspectives of our own that move beyond patriarchy. While men cannot construct feminist theologies, we can attempt to construct postpatriarchal theologies.

A postpatriarchal theology is a conceptual framework that is critical of gender bias and ways of thinking that have accompanied it and that attempts to be constructive of ideas and images intended to point toward ways of living—for women, men, or both—that supersede patriarchy. Feminist theologies are postpatriarchal theologies created by women out of women's experience. Some are intended to be relevant to women alone, others are intended to be relevant to men and to women. Study of both are indispensable for men who wish to construct postpatriarchal religious perspectives.

Three further points must be made. First, at this stage in history, postpatriarchal theologies must be defined by their intentions rather than their achievements. Given the massive inheritance of patriarchal ways of thinking, feeling, and acting, it is doubtful that any theology in the foreseeable future—whether the product of male or female experience—can achieve a total transcendence of patriarchy. At best, it can approximate that transcendence. A postpatriarchal theology is a theology that intends to transcend patriarchy and that in so doing approximates such transcendence.

Second, even as a postpatriarchal theology approximates a transcendence of patriarchy, it utilizes aspects of patriarchy. Inasmuch as a postpatriarchal theology uses language inherited from patriarchal histories, it is inevitably shaped—and sometimes for good—by patriarchy. Transcendence is sometimes a novel synthesis of inherited habits of thinking, feeling, and acting, and sometimes it is a breaking from those ideas and ways of thinking. Even when it breaks from inherited habits, it utilizes aspects of patriarchy to accomplish the breaking.

Third, feminist theologies are by far the most important form of postpatriarchal theology, because women so much better than men can exercise the critical function of postpatriarchal theology. Men are generally too embedded in patriarchal habits to realize them. Their attempts—our attempts—to respond to feminist theologies, particularly when we do constructing on our own, can easily become attempts to coopt feminist theologies: to take over the movement. To counteract this tendency, we must recognize that understanding feminist theologies is indispensable for male-envisioned postpatriarchal perspectives. Feminist theologies are first-order postpatriarchal perspectives; male-envisioned attempts at postpatriarchal thinking are second-order. They follow the lead of feminist perspectives.

As yet, there is no established name for the kind of second-order, constructive theology created by men in response to, and in solidarity with, feminist theologies. There is no generally accepted name for male-envisioned postpatriarchal theology. There is, however, a resource for such theology, and it is to that resource I turn.

II. A Contemporary Example of Postpatriarchal Thinking

The resource is process theology. Of course, previous chapters have dealt with process thought in various contexts. What is interesting for the purposes of this chapter is the fact that process theology has itself been in process. While most but not all of its advocates in the past have been men, increasingly it is being used by women as a resource for developing feminist theologies. The appropriation of process theology for feminist purposes began with Valerie Saiving, one of the pioneers of feminist theology, who used process theology as a way of developing an alternative feminist understanding of the self. In different but overlapping ways, her use of process theology has been complemented and enriched by such feminist thinkers as Rita Nakashima Brock (1988), Sheila Davaney (1981), Nancy Howell (1988), Catherine Keller (1986), Jean Lambert (1981), Lois Livezey (1988), Sallie McFague (1987), Marjorie Suchocki (1982), Penelope Washbourn (1981), and, briefly but interestingly, Dorothee Soelle (1984, 23–27). A few of these theologians would identify themselves as process theologians; most would prefer the ascription "feminist theologian" instead. Nevertheless, all have made constructive use of process theology in developing their feminist theologies, and all have developed feminist points of view that have considerable explicit overlap with process orientations.

What is it, after all, that feminists find helpful about process theology? In most general terms, as Penelope Washbourn explains, it is that both process and feminist thought aim "to revise the fundamental categories of the Western tradition" in similar directions (1981, 85). Both criticize a static, hierarchical mode of social order and advocate in its place an alternative "participatory" social order; both criticize the absolute power of God and propose alternative ways of envisioning the divine; both criticize atomistic understandings of the self and propose instead that the human self is both relational and self-creative; both criticize dualisms between humanity and nature and insist instead that humanity is part of nature; both criticize anthropocentric ethics and emphasize instead the intrinsic value of all living beings, human and nonhuman.

This puts process theology in a unique situation. It seems to offer a conceptual bridge on which women and men can travel separately and, if they wish, together, in conversation with one another, to attempt a move from the shore of patriarchy to that of postpatriarchy. Of course, the bridge itself is being built as it is being traversed. Planks that already have been laid by men may have to be replaced, and many if not most of the planks that have not yet been laid will be laid by women. Moreover, there is no guarantee that even at a conceptual level the other shore will be reached, or that, if reached, it will make a difference in the world. Whether or not process perspectives take hold in seminaries and religious communities remains to be seen. But the journey itself is worth considering, because it offers one example of what a postpatriarchal Christianity, guided by a postpatriarchal theology, might look like.

Christianity as a Changing Tradition

Women and men who are developing process postpatriarchal orientations acknowledge at the outset that a postpatriarchal Christianity—envisioned by process theologians or by other feminist thinkers—is a *new* Christianity. Though it may be influenced by what Rosemary Ruether calls "usable traditions" from the past— both biblical and postbiblical, both orthodox and unorthodox, and both Christian and non-Christian—it creatively synthesizes aspects of these traditions in historically unprecedented ways. Indeed, it involves ways of thinking, feeling, speaking, and acting that cannot be traced to, and that in some respects diverge from, the dominant traditions of the Christian past. The question naturally arises: Is a new Christianity still Christianity?

Process theologians believe that it is. They argue that Christianity always has been, and ought to be, an ongoing process capable of growth and development, rather than a settled and fixed fact destined to repeat its past. It is a historical movement, pluralistic and developmental from its beginnings, rather than a set of timeless abstractions. To participate in this movement is not necessarily to repeat the past; it may well be to help inaugurate a new future.

This is not to suggest that Christians should forget the past. On the contrary, we should remember it, if only not to repeat it. Nor is it to suggest that the past is never worthy of repetition. On the contrary, sometimes it can serve as a resource for, and judge of, the present. For example, there are certainly senses in which subsequent generations of Christians in capitalist societies have fallen from, rather than advanced beyond, the primitive socialism of early Christian communities. And there are many senses in which patriarchal Christians have fallen from, rather than advanced beyond, the more egalitarian Christianity of the original Jesus movement (Fiorenza 1983, 140–154). To say that Christianity is capable of growth is not to say that it has always grown in a positive direction. Sometimes it has regressed, and sometimes subsequent generations have much to learn from prior generations.

To say that Christianity is capable of growth is to say, however, that in the last analysis Christians must evaluate themselves—and determine what is and is not to be called Christian—on the basis of future hopes rather than past achievements. Even when the past is appreciated as a resource, it must be appreciated because it is resourceful for the future, not because it is an unquestionable authority in its own right. To treat it as an unquestionable authority is itself to fall into an idolatry of tradition, therein obstructing the possibility of new life. The authentic Christian life is drawn by an anticipated future rather than propelled by a settled past: a future that is partially realizable in the present, and toward which humans are perpetually beckoned by God. This is a future for which Jesus himself seems to have yearned as he healed the sick and announced good news to the poor. It is a future of shalom: that is, of love and justice among people, of harmony with nature, and of communion with God. This means that in the interests of shalom for women as well as men, and in faithfulness to a God who perpetually beckons toward shalom, Christians can repent—or turn around—from ways of thinking, feeling, and acting that their own predecessors have so often embodied. They can repent from patriarchy and, in so doing, help effect a transformation of the very tradition in which they participate: enabling it to move beyond what it has been toward what it can be.

The development of a postpatriarchal theology is one way, but not the only way, in which this transformation occurs. In addition to new ways of thinking, new forms of worship are also required, as are new ways of speaking and new modes of social interaction. Religion, Christianity included, is much more than theology. Yet theology is important because it helps guide people toward new ways of thinking, feeling, and acting.

III. Six Characteristics of a Postpatriarchal Christianity

In order to understand postpatriarchal modes of thinking, feeling, and acting, we do well to consider six aspects of a postpatriarchal Christianity as understood in a process perspective. It is important to emphasize that these are aspects of a kind of Christianity that can exist in the future. They are aspects of a possible Christianity and of a possible Christian life-style. In the future, so it is hoped, postpatriarchal Christians will embody or emphasize (1) value-pluralistic thinking and care, (2) a logic of relational power, (3) a nondualistic approach to reason and feeling, (4) the self as creative, relational, and dynamic, (5) nature as evolutionary and ecological but not mechanistic, and (6) God as Heart.

The first three features pertain not so much to particular notions concerning the self, world, or God but rather to general dispositions—that is, styles of thinking and modes of feeling—that are encouraged in process postpatriarchal theologies. To understand these three dispositions, recall Karen Warren's argument that in the West a patriarchal mind-set has been disposed toward value-hierarchical thinking, a logic of domination or unilateral power, and certain forms of conceptual dualism. Recall also that she believes these habits of mind have led to an oppression of women and of powerless men, people of "other" races and religions, other animals, and the Earth. Process theologians agree. They point out that classical Christian ways of thinking, including some biblical ways of thinking, have been similarly disposed. They propose for our internalization three alternative dispositions.

Value-Pluralistic Thinking and the Importance of Care

The first can be called "value-pluralistic" thinking. It can best be understood by comparing it to a traditional form of hierarchical thinking in Christianity: namely, the hierarchical thinking that has given rise to Christian exclusivism. Until recently, Catholics have claimed that outside the church there is no salvation; and Protestants have claimed that outside Christianity there is no salvation. To be a Christian has been to hold on to a set of principles and practices labeled "Christian" at the expense of being able to appreciate, and be creatively transformed by, other peoples and other insights. Christianity has been valued "up" at the expense of "other ways" that have been valued "down."

The "others ways" to which Christians have often been closed include, of course, other religions. Traditional Christian attitudes toward Judaism—paving the way for pogrom after pogrom and ultimately leading to the Holocaust—are tragic examples of this intolerance. But Christian intolerance has not been limited to those outside the faith. For men who are Christian, and perhaps for women as well who have internalized the views of men, "other ways" have also included the ways of women. By the "ways of women" I mean the modes of experience and the autonomous interests of women as women, and by intolerance of women I mean androcentrism. Just as the Holocaust shows the effects of excluding the ways of Jews, so European and North American witch burnings show the effects of excluding the ways of women. Both examples indicate that Christianity has been a way that has resisted the acceptance of a plurality of life paths, a diversity of life orientations, a variety of life-styles. As a way characterized by value-hierarchical thinking, Christianity has been a way that excludes other ways.

Process theologians propose by contrast that a postpatriarchal Christianity is a way that excludes no ways. It is disposed to recognize and appreciate a plurality of life paths, life-styles, and life orientations, which is to say that it is inclined toward value-pluralistic thinking over against value-hierarchical thinking. The phrase "Way that excludes no Ways" is borrowed from John Cobb's *Christ in a Pluralistic Age* (1975, 22). In this and other works Cobb proposes that the way of Christianity can and ought to be one in which different forms of value—discovered, among other places, in non-Christian religions, in women, and in nonhuman forms of life—are appreciated, and in which Christians themselves are "creatively transformed" as they recognize and affirm these different values. Indeed, Cobb identifies the living Christ with the creative transformation that emerges out of an embrace of pluralism.

Of course for Cobb, as for all process theologians, there are limits. Tolerance must be a principled tolerance; at some point hierarchical thinking is necessary. Those life orientations that promote the well-being of women as well as men, for example, are to be judged higher, and more worthy of affirmation, than those that promote men at the expense of women. But there can be many life-enhancing life orientations: African as well as Asian, Latin American as well as North American, Oceanic as well as European, rural as well as urban, homosexual as well as heterosexual, female as well as male. None of these ways need be absolutized; all have capacities for evil as well as good. Yet each can have beauty and integrity in its own right, and each can add something to our own lives and to the divine Life. A postpatriarchal Christianity is a way that hierarchicalizes as a last, not a first, resort.

It is out of this desire not to exclude others that a deep concern for justice emerges in postpatriarchal Christianity. To be open to other people is not simply to acknowledge their right to exist; it is to be influenced by them. It is to listen to others, to hear them on their own terms, to imaginatively feel their feelings, to share in their destinies, and to revision one's own perspective with theirs in mind. A postpatriarchal Christianity is one that is particularly open to those who are excluded by the societies in which they live: the victims, the outcasts, the forgotten, the unwanted, the marginalized, the despised, the poor. The natural consequence of such openness is a hunger for justice, for people of course, and also for humanly abused animals and for the Earth. This hunger originates not from abstract principles understood to derive from an inscrutable God or from a transcendent rationality, though its application may be guided from some understanding of God or by the demands of reason. Rather, it originates from a sense of connectedness with those who suffer and from an appreciation of the value of life. It issues from care (Noddings 1984).

Care of this sort has often been identified with "the feminine" in the West. Feminists rightly object to this stereotype because they recognize that the stereotype has given a one-sided and distorted notion of women's capacities, and because it has been created primarily by men for their own benefit. In fact "the feminine" in the West, like "the feminine" in many other cultures, has been male-defined; it has been the "patriarchal feminine." Postpatriarchal Christians need not dwell on the question of whether care is feminine or masculine. Instead they can propose that it is, or can be, human: a capacity for subjective responsiveness to others that can and should be embodied by women and by men.

Relational Power

A life of care is by no means powerless, at least given the notion of "power" that postpatriarchal Christians find most meaningful. Recall that according to Karen Warren the kind of power emphasized in Western patriarchy is unilateral power: the power to be in complete control over another while being minimally influenced in the process. Feminists such as Susan Griffin (1979) insist that this is the power which men have desired to exercise over women and nature. They propose, as do process theologians, that another kind of power is more desirable and more in touch with the ultimate nature of reality.

In process theology this alternative form of power is called relational power or, as Rita Nakashima Brock speaks of it, following Huanani-Kay Trask and others, "erotic power" (Brock 1988, 25). Such power is not a commodity to be exercised over and against others, as if its increase in one person required a decrease in others. Rather, it is something that "creates and connects hearts," something that "involves the whole person in relationships of self-awareness, vulnerability, openness, and caring" (1988, 26). It is "erotic" because it is imbued with eros, a yearning to be as richly related to others as is possible and therein to discover the fullness of life. A postpatriarchal Christianity will emphasize that women and men can find fulfillment in and through the exercise of relational rather than unilateral power, which has two inseparable aspects.[1]

First, it is a power to creatively receive influences from the past, other people, and the surrounding world. It is noteworthy that *Webster's Ninth New Collegiate Dictionary* gives one definition of "power" as the ability to be influenced or to undergo an effect. This understanding of power—the power to receive influences—is generally neglected in modern English parlance because for us the word "power" ordinarily connotes an act of exercising control over others. Despite the distortion of the word "power" by the image of control, however, we recognize a kind of strength in those people whose minds are so open that they can receive and then creatively integrate many different intellectual influences or whose hearts are so open that they can hear and understand different kinds of people without being narrow and intolerant. We recognize a strength in those who can feel deeply, who can share in the sufferings and joys of others, who can affirm the uniqueness of the gift of each individual as an added dimension of richness in their own lives. This strength is the receptive side of relational power. It is the power to be open-minded and open-hearted and to be changed in the process. As the very antithesis of defensiveness, it is the strength to be creatively vulnerable.

Relational power is, in its second aspect, the power to determine one's own destiny, to express oneself creatively, and therein to influence others. Here relational power bears a family resemblance to unilateral power because it, like unilateral power, affects the world. Yet it differs in a very important way. Unilateral power has as its aim the control of others in a way that subverts their own creativity and minimizes their opportunities for reciprocal influence. By contrast, relational power has as its aim the influencing of others in a way that appreciates and inspires their creativity and invites reciprocal influence.

In order to understand the active side of relational power, consider Alice Walker's novel *The Color Purple*. Unilateral power is the power that Celie's dominating and abusive husband had over her; relational power is the power that Shug, Celie's newfound lover, had with her. Those who have read the novel will recognize that Shug was by no means a weak, nonassertive person. She had a powerful effect on Celie. Yet her power in relation to Celie was not a power that sought or obtained control. Rather, it was a power to creatively influence Celie in a way that inspired Celie's own creative response. It was a power to empower Celie and to be empowered by the unpredictability of Celie's response.

The role of surprise—of unpredictability—in relational power is important. Whereas in unilateral power the good to be achieved in the exercise of control is predicted in advance by the one seeking the control, thus limiting outcomes, in relational power the good to be achieved emerges out of the relationship itself. For this reason a central feature of relational power amid human interactions is risk:

the risk that, if one is not in complete control of the other, richer experiences can emerge for oneself and the other than if one is in control. Fear is the primary obstacle to such risk.

Postpatriarchal Christians need not hope for a world in which the exercise of unilateral control is entirely eliminated. Some degree of unilateral power is inevitable in human relations and in relations between humanity and the rest of nature. Rather, they can hope for a world in which relational power is maximized and unilateral power minimized. They can hope for a world in which "true power"—that is, the most desirable form of power—includes vulnerability as well as creativity, dependence as well as self-expression, being affected as well as affecting. Such power, as will be suggested subsequently, is concordant with divine power.

Nondualistic Thinking and the Importance of Feeling

In addition to emphasizing value-pluralistic thinking and relational power, postpatriarchal Christians will emphasize nondualistic thinking. This does not mean that they oppose all distinctions. One can think nondualistically and yet make important distinctions between things: say, between the psyche and the body or between God and the world. To emphasize nondualistic thinking is to oppose the assumption that the "things" to be distinguished are atomistic, and hence that they exist in mutual independence from one another, or at least that one of them exists in absolute independence from the other. Dualistic thinking is atomistic thinking, polarized thinking.

The alternative is nondualistic, or relational, thinking. To think in this way is to recognize that logically and, indeed, ontologically any given actuality—whether material or psychological, secular or sacred, human or nonhuman, terrestrial or celestial—exists in relation to, and hence in partial dependence on, countless other actualities. This recognition is profoundly Buddhist, and it is also, at least from the vantage point of some scientists, profoundly scientific. It is no accident that in developing their theological orientations process theologians have been shaped by, and indebted to, insights from Asia, from modern biology, and from modern physics. Along with most Buddhists and many scientists, process thinkers submit that there are no independent substances, no self-enclosed atoms, no isolated "things." While human beings and other animals are partially self-determining, their self-determination lies not in transcending influences but rather in integrating influences. Even freedom is freedom in relation. To think nondualistically is to recognize the radically relational character of all existents and thus to move beyond the many dualisms that have characterized so much of patriarchal Christianity.

The process emphasis on nondualistic thinking has implications even for the way in which thinking is conceived, at least if by "thinking" we mean reason and if by "reason" we mean discursive reason. Among the many dualisms that process and feminist theologians propose to overcome in the interests of a postpatriarchal Christianity is that between reason and feeling. In the West reason has often been conceived as a cognitive activity independent of, rather than dependent upon, feeling. It has been presumed (1) that rational thought is itself a relatively nonaffective activity, devoid of passion, intuition, or emotion, and (2) that feeling and emotion have no cognitive content. These presuppositions have affected the ways in which men and women are approached because masculinity has often been identified with autonomous rational thought and femininity with nonautonomous vulnerable feeling.

Process theologians propose alternatives to each of the above-mentioned assumptions. They suggest, in the first place, that reason itself is infused with forms of feeling. Whenever one reasons, one "feels" the presence of ideas, amid which one "enjoys" their clarity, or is "perplexed" by their ambiguity, or "appreciates" their aesthetic richness, or "judges" them to be false, or "intuits" their truth value. Enjoyment, perplexity, appreciation, judgment, and intuition are forms of feeling that are responsive to images and ideas. In their own way, they are no less affective than those forms of feeling that respond to sense perception. Rational affections differ from other forms in that the data to which they respond are "internal" rather than "external," mental rather than physical.

Furthermore, process theologians suggest that nondiscursive feelings—that is, feelings that are not emotional responses to abstract ideas—can have cognitive value in their own right. Consider, for example, the many feelings that accompany our perceptions of the natural world: feelings of beauty and wonder, mystery and awe, fear and delight. In an intuitive way we learn something about nature through such feelings, even though they are not immediately amenable to intellectualized abstractions or controlled by rational processes. Consider also the feelings that absorb us in dreams, when we are open to preconscious and prereflective dimensions of experience. Here too we learn something about nature: namely, the nature of our own subconscious minds. A process epistemology includes more than reason among its avenues for knowing. As David Griffin explains, "Human experience is not limited to sensory and conscious experience, and human knowing includes not only intellectual operations but also affective, aesthetic, symbolic, imaginal, and bodily operations, which are equally important" (1987b, 7; see also Muray 1988, 123–136).

Griffin's description of human cognition is meant to be free from gender bias. As with all process thinkers, he believes that for men and for women, knowing is—or can be—affective, aesthetic, symbolic, imaginal, and bodily, as well as rational. A postpatriarchal Christianity emphasizes the cultivation of each and all of these forms of knowledge.

The Human Self as Creative, Relational, and Dynamic

Of course, human beings are more than knowers. They are experiencers, and there is more to being an experiencer than knowing. In the life of an experiencer there is doing, willing, hoping, trusting, fearing, dreaming, yearning, breathing, loving, remembering, forgetting, laughing, crying, and dying. Whether or not these experiences have cognitive value, they are the very content of an individual life as lived from the inside. When enjoyed, they have aesthetic value even if they lack cognitive value. The question naturally arises: What is it—or, better, who is it—that suffers or enjoys these experiences? What or who is the human self? A postpatriarchal Christianity must arrive at some way of viewing the human self that is relevant to the experiences and possibilities of women and men.

Here the work of one process feminist, Catherine Keller, is particularly helpful. In *From a Broken Web: Separation, Sexism, and Self* (1986), Keller points out that in patriarchal Christianity, as in so much of the West, the self has often been construed in nonrelational, atomistic terms. It has been construed as a soul cut off from the world by the boundaries of the skin, or, in post-Christian settings, as a "mind" that resides in the body separated from an "objective" world. This way of conceiving the self—as an atomized, autonomous, disembodied, unrelational substance of one sort or another—has had destructive consequences for both women and men.

For men it has been destructive in that it has supported the psychological ideal of complete autonomy, which has itself inhibited the realization of possibilities for intimacy and equality. An atomistic understanding of selfhood has undergirded the idea that a man is to achieve his authentic identity only if he is clearly distinguishable from others and from the surrounding world. The concept of the isolated ego has codified the idea that only separation—under the banners of "independence" and "autonomy"—prepares the way for authentic existence. Drawing from the work of Nancy Chodorow (1978), Keller speculates that in Western societies the impulse for separation in males may stem from the early age at which young boys have had to separate themselves from their mothers. The conception of self as isolated ego may itself be a projection of the male experience of the separated self. The style of experience can change only after the social structures have changed.

For women, the conception of self as isolated ego has had destructive consequences in two ways. First, as embodied by men, it has led to the view of women as "other." Of course, there are important senses in which women *are* "other" in relation to men. Men must learn to recognize that individual women—and perhaps women in general—have unique values as women, values "other" than those readily realized or realizable by men. But the "otherness" of such value is not what I am speaking about here. Rather, I am speaking of the "otherness" of being an object upon whom unilateral power is exercised, the otherness of an object to be controlled. When men have been influenced by the ideal of the autonomous self, they have approached women as objects to be controlled by that self.

The second way in which the conception of self as isolated ego has had destructive consequences for women pertains not so much to the adoption of this conceptuality by men as to its adoption or counteradoption by women. If the only option for conceiving self is that of the isolated ego, a woman is in a double bind. On the one hand, she can be a patriarchal self, in which case, like a man, she seeks to become separate from the world: an autonomous ego cut off from the world by the boundaries of her skin. Or, on the other hand, she can think of herself in opposite and complementary terms: as an utterly relational self whose sole value lies in being of service to, and dependent on, others, and whose primary ideal is self-sacrifice or selflessness. In the latter instance, which is more common under patriarchal circumstances, she becomes the counterpart to the male ego: the one possessed by the possessor. Keller speaks of this counterpart as the "soluble" self: that is, the self that has been dissolved into relational bondage.

Keller recognizes that in response to the dilemmas of a soluble self, women often seem to opt for an autonomous ego. "Often we hear women say that first, or finally, they must get separate individuality and develop their own autonomy: an especially pressing motive among women coming up to breathe after long immersion in marriages, families, and disappointing love affairs" (1986, 3). From the point of view of an observer, and perhaps from the point of view of a woman herself, to get "separate individuality" can be to assume a traditionally masculine ego pattern. But Keller does not believe that this is the actual aim of most women who seek autonomy. She does not believe that most women, in seeking "an empowering center in themselves and often furious at the sums of selfhood drained away in futile asymmetries, are actually repudiating connectedness." Rather they "desire worlds—places of inner and outer freedom in which new forms of connection can take place." Their hope is that in these worlds they can "range through an unlimited array of relations—not just to other persons, but to ideas and feeling, to the earth, the body, and the untold contents of the pressing moment." In other words, "women struggling against the constraints of conventionally feminine modes of relation desire not less but more (and different) relation: not disconnection, but connection that counts" (1986, 3).

The image of self as autonomous ego does not allow for this "connection that counts." Given the inadequacy of the image for women and for men, Keller says that "something new is needed" (1986, 4). Using process categories of thought, she offers an alternative way of conceiving the self that eliminates the double bind for women and provides a more hopeful option for men. It is to think of the self as an ongoing, multifaceted, and everchanging process of experiencing, each moment of which is, in its depths, a creative synthesis of many worlds. In order to understand this, consider diagrams 1 and 2.

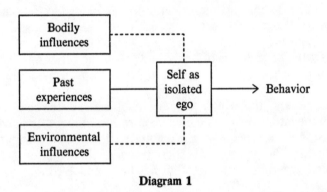

Diagram 1

Diagram 1 illustrates the "autonomous ego" view of the self. Here the self is represented by a self-enclosed box that has an identity—an internal space—apart from its relations to its body and the environment. Those who think this way generally recognize that the self is conditioned by the body, by the extrabodily environment (including other people, artifacts, plants and animals, land, and the atmosphere), and by past experiences. The lines leading from the phrases "environmental influences," "bodily influences," and "past experiences" represent these influences. However, at least with respect to the extrabodily environment and perhaps also the body, advocates of the autonomous ego generally understand this conditioning on the analogy of two self-enclosed billiard balls colliding with a third called the "self." The self they envision is not internally related to the environment or the body, such that its connections with the body and the environment are internal to its own identity. Rather, it is externally related to the body and the environment, which is to say that it could "be what it is" even if those relations were different. The fact that the influence lines leading from environment and body are broken rather than solid represents the fact that these relations are external to the identity of the self rather than internal. In principle, the self with its own past experiences could be transplanted into a new body and a new environment and still be the same self.

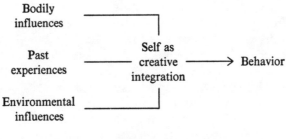

Diagram 2

Diagram 2 illustrates Keller's alternative to this way of thinking. Here the self is no longer self-enclosed. The lines leading from the body, the environment, and past experiences are each solid, representing the fact that the self's relations to these realities are internal to its own identity and existence. Moreover, these relations are not simply causal connections discerned by an objective observer from a third-person perspective. They are feelings enjoyed or suffered from a first-person perspective. From Keller's point of view the self "feels" or "takes into account" body, environment, and past experiences, both consciously and subconsciously, and in so doing is "connected" with them. Not just the feelings, but the items felt, enter into the self's own constitution, becoming part of its own identity. The environment and the body are just as much a part of the self as are the self's own past experiences. From this perspective it would make no sense to speak of the "self" being transplanted into a new body and yet remaining unchanged in the process. In a new body, or a new world, the self is a new and different self.

To emphasize the relationality of Keller's perspective, however, is to tell only half the story. For her as for all process thinkers, the self is not simply a synthesis of connections to body, environment, and past experiences; it is a *creative* synthesis of these relations. If an omniscient observer knew all the factors from the body, the environment, and the past that were going to influence the self, that observer could not predict with absolute certainty how the synthesis would occur or what the behavioral outcome of it would be. In the depths of the self there is an act of decision: an act of cutting off certain possibilities for integrating "the many into one" and therein actualizing other possibilities. This decision, too, is part of the self. The self's creativity lies not in being independent of connections with others but in creatively determining the quality and style of that dependence. Freedom is "how" many influences become one self. To be free is to be creatively dependent.

Both because the self is free and because it is profoundly dependent on changing circumstances, the self is itself fluid and dynamic. The self is not a settled and static "thing" or "entity" that owns or possesses feelings and decisions. Rather, it is an ongoing process of feeling and deciding from one second to the next, one minute to the next, one hour to the next, one day to the next. As soon as a given moment of creative synthesis occurs, it becomes a past experience to be integrated by successive instances of creative synthesis. Thus a person's sense of continuity over time is largely a function of memory. In fact the self is a verb rather than a noun, a pilgrimage rather than a destination, a journey rather than a stopping place. From this perspective one can never step into the same river twice, not simply because the river changes but because the self changes.

The fact that the self can and does change—that its very existence and identity can be different from one moment to the next—means that people can grow beyond their pasts, can become new persons. This is important for women and men who seek existences and identities different from those into which they have been conditioned by patriarchy. These women and men can never become absolutely disconnected from their pasts, but they can creatively integrate those past influences in ways that transcend their destructive power.

Keller believes that the process model of the human self is true to the nature of human existence, including women's experience. She agrees with Sheila Davaney, who writes that "the process perspective reflects and affirms the feminist understanding of women as subjects" (1981, 4). Both agree that human subjects are creative and relational and that the image of the self as an isolated ego is ontologically misguided.

Yet from Keller's perspective, as from that of Davaney, ontology is by no means the most important issue. A creative-relational view of the self commends itself, not simply because it approximates truth concerning the way things are but because it offers a promising human ideal for the way things can be. The ideal is to live a life consistent with the very nature of the self. It is to be, and allow others to be, creatively relational. Of course, not just any relations will do. The relations must be "connections that count." Such connections involve relational power rather than unilateral power, and they involve mutual care. Keller's hope—and that of a postpatriarchal

Christianity—is that women and men alike can enjoy "connections that count" without discrimination on the basis of gender.

More than that, the hope is that women and men can enjoy such connections in and through healthy affirmations of their own genders. Part of what must be integrated into the life of a creative and relational self is gender itself. For most of us, gender identity is partly the result of our body chemistry, partly the result of social conditioning, and partly the result of decisions we have made in the past and are making in the present. How much our gender is the result of body chemistry and how much the result of social conditioning is a matter of serious and important debate. What is important to add, however, is that regardless of the outcome of this debate, freedom also plays a role. At least in part, we choose what it means "to be a man" or "to be a woman." As Mary Daly's appropriation of words like "hag" and "bitch" attests, inherited meanings of "woman" can be changed, by women themselves, in which case the very meaning of "being a woman" changes. In the life of a given individual, and in the life of a society, gender identity can evolve. Keller and other process theologians propose that there may well be "new ways of being male" and "new ways of being female" that we ourselves, in the immediacy of the present, can begin to create.

Nature as Evolutionary and Ecological, but Not Mechanistic

The human self as described in the previous section is inseparable from nature. To say that the human self is partly free is not to suggest that the self is supernatural. Rather, it is to invite a nonmechanistic way of conceiving nature: a way that sees human freedom as a sophisticated evolutionary expression of, rather than a sophistical exception to, what is happening in other animals, in living cells, and in the depths of submicroscopic matter. In a process postpatriarchal theology, as in most forms of feminist theology, other biological organisms too are creative, relational, and dynamic. The natural world is evolutionary and ecological but not mechanistic.

The affirmation that nature is not mechanistic has important implications for a postpatriarchal religious orientation. The underlying metaphor of the mechanistic worldview is that nature is *like a machine,* which is to say that it is like a vast assemblage of lifeless, atomized particles in motion that can and should be used exclusively for the ends of human beings. In *The Death of Nature: Women, Ecology, and the Scientific Revolution,* the historian of science Carolyn Merchant explains how this metaphor functioned in the scientific revolutions of the sixteenth and seventeenth centuries to sanction an exploitation of nature, unfettered commercial expansion, and a new socioeconomic order that subordinated women. Merchant reminds us that under the dominance of this metaphor nature was approached—in the words of Francis Bacon—as something to be "bound into service" and made a "slave." And she reminds us that much of the imagery Bacon used in articulating the objectives and methods of the new science derived from the witch trials of his day. Under the scrutiny of science, Bacon implied, mother nature is to be hounded in her wanderings much as witches are to be hounded in their wanderings. Both were to be subdued, interrogated, and conquered (Merchant 1985, 169).

Despite revolutions in science in our century, the metaphor of nature as machine prevails in much science today. As Merchant puts it, "The mechanistic approach to nature is as fundamental to the twentieth-century revolution in physics as it was to classical Newtonian science" (1985, 291). This means that contemporary science, despite its many accomplishments, often advances a way of thinking that continues to have a destructive effect on human and nonhuman life. Illustrative of this destruction of nonhuman life is the fact that 100 to 200 million nonhuman animals die each year in scientific laboratories around the world, oftentimes under conditions of severe stress and pain, with little protest from within the global scientific community (Ryder 1975). The animals are dispatched, in part, because they are implicitly viewed as machines that can be "bound into service" for human ends. Today science plays no small role in encouraging a mechanistic understanding of life.

Like process theologians, Merchant believes there is a viable and socially necessary alternative to the machine metaphor. She argues that the human future—and that of the Earth and its creatures as well—may depend on our learning to see and think of nature as a living organism rather than as a machine (1985, 289). She points to the philosophy of Whitehead as an important example of what it might mean in a contemporary context to understand nature organically rather than mechanistically. It is by this Whiteheadian alternative that process postpatriarchal theologies are deeply shaped.

While advocating an organic rather than mechanistic understanding of nature, process theologies are by no means antiscientific. Indeed, they are deeply influenced, among other things, by evolutionary thinking. From astrophysicists and cosmologists, process theologians have learned to affirm, and to integrate into a religious orientation, the idea that the universe as we know it is the result of a ten- to twenty-billion-year process of cosmic evolution, and that this process continues into the present. And from evolutionary biologists they have learned to affirm, and again to integrate into their religious orientation, the idea that life on Earth as we know it is also the result of an evolutionary process that continues into the present. Moreover, they recognize with at least some speculative physicists that there may well be other forms of life on other planets surrounding other stars, and they insist, as do most biologists, that even in terms of life on Earth there is no reason to assume that human life is the exclusive aim or goal of the biological process. A process postpatriarchal Christianity recognizes that human beings are by no means the sole locus of value or the sole end of cosmic and terrestrial evolutionary developments. All living beings, not just human beings, have intrinsic value.

In addition to being influenced by evolutionary theories, process theology is influenced by quantum mechanics and relativity theories in physics, by ecology and cognitive ethology in biology, and by thermodynamics in physical chemistry. Indeed, most process theologians submit that a dialogue between religion and science, in which religious perspectives are partially shaped by insights from science, is essential to the very future of religion. A postpatriarchal Christianity must be a scientifically informed Christianity.

Yet the dialogue with science is, and must be, two-way. Even as postpatriarchal Christians learn from science, they can and should be critical of the mechanistic worldview by which so much practicing science has been motivated. The argument of process thinkers such as John Cobb, Charles Birch, and David Griffin is that science can proceed in terms of, and indeed be advanced by, an alternative, organic worldview such as that proposed by Whitehead. In so doing, science would itself contribute more richly to that liberation of life which is sorely needed in our time. We would have a "reenchanted" science (see Griffin 1987b; 1988).

For life to be liberated, then, process theologians believe the very concept of life must be liberated from the mechanistic interpretation to which it has often been subjected in the natural sciences. In a process context the word "mechanistic" refers to one or some combination of the following five perspectives: (1) a deterministic perspective in which present happenings are understood to be entirely determined by causative powers from the past, (2) a utilitarian perspective in which the value of living things is understood to be purely instrumental rather than intrinsic, (3) a devitalized perspective in which the depths of physical matter are understood to be lifeless and inert rather than lifelike and creative, (4) a reductionistic perspective in which living wholes are understood to be utterly reducible to nonliving parts, and (5) a dualistic perspective in which sharp dichotomies are drawn between spirit and matter, supernatural and natural, mind and body, thought and feeling, self and world. At a conceptual level, to say that nature is like a machine is to think in terms of one or several of these points of view.

The organic worldview advocated by process thinkers stresses alternative ideas, some of which include insights from mechanism and some of which contravene mechanistic perspectives. Process thinkers emphasize (1) that present happenings emerge not only out of causative powers from the past but also from creative impulses in the present guided by final causes from the future. This means that nonhuman organisms, like human beings, are partially creative, and hence partially unpredictable, in the ways in which they respond to, and integrate, environmental and bodily influences. In addition, process thinkers propose (2) that nonhuman organisms—from living cells to porpoises—are of intrinsic value in and for themselves even as they are of instrumental importance to others, (3) that physical matter itself is more alive than dead in its ultimate depths, (4) that living wholes, such as the human self or an animal psyche, are very much influenced by, and yet more than, the parts of which they are composed, and (5) that reality itself, while in many respects pluralistic and manifold in its domains and dimensions, is better characterized as interdependent and interfusing than as dualistic and dichotomized. In the latter respect, the process understanding of nature is very similar to a Buddhist orientation. For process thinkers as for Buddhists, nature is a seamless web of interdependent realities, of which we are a part.

It is important to note that some scientists today—David Bohm (1980) in physics, for example; Ilya Prigogine (1984) in physical chemistry; and Donald Griffin (1984) in biology—have already adopted aspects of an organic orientation. This suggests that the concept of nature in science itself may be changing in ways intimated by process thinkers. It is precisely this kind of creative transformation in science that can and should parallel creative transformations in religion. A postpatriarchal Christianity can best be complemented by a postpatriarchal—that is, a postmechanistic—science.

God as Heart

Women and men seeking liberation from male rule are no less part of living nature, and no less part of evolution, than other living beings, both human and nonhuman. And they, like other creatures, are drawn by goals or purposes for living with some degree of satisfaction relative to the situation at hand. In the case of postpatriarchal Christians, the situation at hand is and has been patriarchy. The goal is to live with greater satisfaction than that which has been available under patriarchy. Christians and others rightly name this satisfaction shalom, that dynamic and relational peace that is the fullness of life in relation to other people, nonhuman nature, and the divine Spirit.

The five characteristics of a postpatriarchal Christianity just mentioned are strategies for achieving a meaningful approximation of shalom in the world. They are also characteristics of human life that might sustain shalom once it is approximated. I submit that shalom can be approached and sustained (1) if Christians and others begin to embody value-pluralistic thinking and its affective undergirding, care, (2) if they begin to cherish and embody relational power more than unilateral power, (3) if they cultivate the art of nondualistic thinking and realize its inseparability from feeling, (4) if they learn to see the self as creative and relational rather than as an isolated ego, and (5) if they learn to appreciate, with the help of a postmechanistic science, the natural world as organic and evolutionary.

The hope for shalom is not necessarily a hope for life after death although, as I suggested in the first chapter, it can involve such hope. To hope for shalom can involve a desire that living beings—pelicans, for example—are redeemed after death. Still, it is not death itself that is the evil. Rather, it is the incompleteness, the absence of wholeness, that leads us to hope that, at least for the myriad beings who die in incompleteness, death is not the final story.[2] The quest for postpatriarchal existence is a quest not for quantity of existence beyond finitude but for quality of existence, be it in this life or, if such exists, in the next.

What motivates the quest for such quality? Among humans and other living beings as well, many are motivated by the necessity of finding an option to intolerable situations under patriarchy. The motivation is to escape suffering. But process theologians suggest that there is something else at work. People are also motivated by the possibility of shalom itself as experienced within the depths of their own subjective experience. This is the beckoning light, a still small voice, that was discussed in the first and succeeding chapters: that inwardly felt lure toward self-actualization—including gender affirmation—in community with other people, other living beings, the Earth, and the divine Spirit. As chapter 1 emphasized, this lure is also present in nonhuman organisms as that by which they are inspired to live from moment to moment with some degree of satisfaction relative to their situations. This lure is God, or at least the active side of God.

Feminists influenced by process theology disagree on whether or not the word "God" can be used in a postpatriarchal Christian setting. For some—Rita Nakashima Brock (1988) and Catherine Keller (1986), for example—the word is too tainted with images of an exclusively masculine deity, or a cosmic moralist, or an all-powerful autocrat to be useful. For others—Marjorie Suchocki (1982), for example—the word is still a helpful and at present indispensable word for naming the sacred reality. But all agree that the sacred reality itself is not exclusively male, nor is it a cosmic moralist or an all-powerful autocrat. And they agree that whether or not the word

"God" is used, other words—new and different words—are also needed to name the sacred reality: words such as lover and friend, light and life, mother and daughter, water and fire, earth and eros. Christians and others are at a stage in which experimentation in naming and describing God is required and in which, for some, the very word "God" must be abandoned.

Amid this experimentation, a word that may be particularly help-ful, which I have used earlier and upon which I focus in drawing this work to a close, is "heart." I submit that in a postpatriarchal context the divine mystery can be named, and felt, as Heart. In postpatriar-chal theologies influenced by process perspectives, the word "heart" has been used most systematically and creatively by Brock. Brock uses the word to refer not to the divine as such but rather to the holistic dimensions of self. She speaks of patriarchy as a state of being brokenhearted and of postpatriarchy as a yearning for, and an inter-nalization of, relational power as incarnate in our own hearts. Be-cause in process theology the divine mystery is the most inclusive example of relational power, Heart—with an uppercase *H*—can name this mystery.

Heart is meant to complement and enrich other words tradition-ally used in process theology to name the divine mystery: phrases such as "the cosmic Mind" or "the Self who includes all selves" or "the divine Consciousness" or "the all-inclusive Self" or "the Lure." It can also complement and enrich, though not replace, more per-sonal metaphors such as "Mother" and "Father," "Lover" and "Friend." Consider how it can complement the description of God as cosmic Mind or Self. Recall that in previous chapters God has been described as a universal, omnipresent Subject who feels and responds to the worldly events as they occur and whose very subjec-tivity is an ever-changing and yet ever-constant creative integration of worldly events. In this sense God is a Self who includes, and is affected by, all selves. Just as a human self creatively integrates bodily influences, such that what happens in the body happens in the self, so the divine Self creatively integrates everything that happens in the universe, such that what happens in the universe happens in the divine Self. God can be imagined as the mind of the universe, so I have suggested, and the universe as the body of God.

If "mind" is understood as an embodied and relational mind, as is the case in process theology, the mind-body analogy has distinct advantages over patriarchal ways of thinking about God. Still, as Brock points out, the mind-body analogy may itself have disadvan-tages, at least if "mind" suggests reason divorced from feeling or thought divorced from care. In this case the word "mind" itself is too cold, too masculine, too oriented toward logos at the expense of eros, too patriarchal. Naming God "Heart" can function to complement, if not to replace, the language of God as Mind. Recall the point made in the first chapter, that according to the *Oxford English Dictionary,* heart refers to mind in the widest sense, including the functions of feeling and will as well as intellect (1970, 159). The true intentions of process thought can be better realized if we speak of God as the Heart of the universe and universe as the body of this Heart.

The word "heart" has several additional meanings and associations that tell us something about the divine as understood in a process context. One meaning is "center of vital functions" or "seat of life" or "life itself." When, for example, we say that "our hearts were gladdened" by some good news, or when we speak of going somewhere with "our heart in our hands," we mean by "heart" our innermost being, the center of our lives, our life itself. In a process context the divine lure is indeed the seat of life in the sense of being that within each being by which the very will to live with satisfaction and wholeness is elicited. It is no accident that in their work at the interface of theology and biology Charles Birch and John Cobb speak of the divine mystery as the Life—with an uppercase *L*—by which all other lives—with a lowercase *l*—are enlivened. To speak of the divine mystery as Heart is to highlight its connection with life.

A second meaning of heart is "center" or "core" or "middle." We speak of getting to "the heart of the matter," and by this we mean getting to the center of an issue, the middle of it. As a metaphor for God, Heart rightly suggests that the divine mystery is at the core or center of the universe and of life itself, rather than above or outside it. This need not imply that the divine mystery is not in some ways transcendent. Indeed, from a process perspective the mystery *is* transcendent. It is a relational Self—with consciousness, purposes, creativity, and care—who includes all selves. Yet this Self is within us, in the center of our lives, and not simply outside us or external to us. We can experience divine transcendence not only as an external authority over against us but also, and perhaps primarily, as an inexhaustible font of possibilities within us: a wellspring of beckoning potentialities by which, if we are creatively responsive, our lives and those of others are fulfilled. Sin is missing the mark of responding to these possibilities, missing the mark of responding to God within us. God within us is the Heart of our hearts.

A third way in which the word "heart" is used is to refer to inner feelings of sympathy, understanding, compassion, and care. We speak of caring people as being "full of heart," and by this we mean they have deep love and affection for others. For process thinkers the divine mystery is heartful in this sense in two ways. The cosmic Heart is active in the world as an inwardly felt lure, which is one way its love is expressed. It is also receptive of the world as an all-empathic consciousness, which is the other way its love is realized. It is bipolar, both yin and yang. In its bipolarity, Heart is the ultimate expression of relational power. It is potentially the most influential power in the universe though the efficacy of its influence depends on worldly response, and it is the most vulnerable power in the universe. In the latter respect Heart feels the feelings of living beings, suffering their sufferings, enjoying their joys, sharing in their destinies in ways much deeper than we can imagine. Moreover, it does so in a pluralistic way. Its empathy is responsive to each individual life on its own terms: to the amoeba on its terms, to the pelican on its terms, and to a human being on her or his terms. The divine mystery is "all heart," not only because it is imbued with empathy but also because it is receptive of diversity. It is the Heart that includes all hearts.

Inasmuch as it is responsive to living beings on their own terms, and inasmuch as humans are among the beings to which it is responsive, the divine Heart is personal as well as transpersonal. It can be referred to as "he" or "she" as well as "it." As described above, I have used "it," in part to avoid gender bias. But the language of "he" or "she" can be used as well. In different contexts and for different people, either or both of these words may be meaningful. Certainly for some the image of a tender, caring Father—the "Abba" addressed by Jesus—can still be helpful. Fathers, too, can have heart. For many postpatriarchal Christians, however, "she" may well be more appropriate than "he," given the history of patriarchal God-language in the West. In fact the divine Heart bears much greater resemblance to the creative and relational self envisioned by feminists such as Catherine Keller than it does to the autonomous ego celebrated, for example, by existentialist philosophies. God is indeed strong, but that strength is tender, and it lies in being creatively relational rather than in being absolutely independent. For those who have been oppressed by patriarchal imagery or who have used such imagery to oppress others, the divine Spirit is best conceived not as a father who art in heaven, but rather as a mother, lover, and friend (McFague 1987, 97–187).

For process thinkers, the life well lived is one that is open to the divine Heart. Openness of this sort is faith, and it is an art rather than a science. It involves trust in a Presence who cannot be manipulated through conscious control and whose depths cannot be fully exhausted by conceptual formulas or religious doctrines. The fruits of openness include value-pluralistic thinking, care for others, a hunger for justice, the enjoyment of relational power, a union of thought and feeling, a discovery of one's self as creatively integrative, an appreciation of nature as organic and evolutionary, and a reverence for life.

Postpatriarchal theologies within Christianity are a promising sign that such transformation can occur in at least one religion. In this chapter I have explained the nature and function of postpatriarchal theology, and I have illustrated one version of it: a process postpatriarchal perspective. In fact, within Christianity and elsewhere, many versions of postpatriarchal theologies are needed: some created by women, some by men, and some created jointly. Furthermore, if these changes in religious self-understanding are to influence society, they must be complemented and enriched by new ways of thinking that emerge in other sectors of society, including scientific communities. In our time the lure of the divine Heart is itself a beckoning toward new, imaginative visions that elicit compassion as well as understanding. "Where there is no vision," the Bible tells us, "the people perish" (Prov. 29:18, KJV). The question of our age is whether such vision will emerge in time to stem the tides of ecological destruction, social injustice, and war. I believe that the ways of thinking endorsed in this work can help. It can help to think in terms of a God who loves pelicans, to adopt an ethic that stresses reverence for life, to practice a spirituality that stresses the interdependence of all things, and to move in thought and deed toward a postpatriarchal Christianity. It is good for us, and for God, that the future is open to such possibilities.

Notes

Introduction

1. For information concerning the cruel treatment of animals in factory farms, see Singer (1975, 92–162); and for information concerning the abuse of animals in scientific laboratories, see Ryder (1975; 1985). Enlightening studies of endangered and extinct species, and of the human role in precipitating rates of species extinction, include Day (1981) and Ehrlich (1981, 103–176). Among the many sources to understanding the contemporary abuse of the Earth, the work of the World Resources Institute (1988) and the World Commission on Environment and Development (1987) are particularly helpful.

2. The words are from a popular Christian hymn in Malawi. They were taught to me by Trudy and Harvey Sindima. As translated by the Sindimas, the lyrics are:

> Jesu, Jesu
> Fill us with your love
> Show us how to serve
> The neighbors we have from you.
>
> Neighbors are rich people and poor
> Neighbors are black people and white
> Neighbors are nearby and far away.
>
> This is the way we should love
> This is the way we should live
> This is the way we should serve the world.
>
> Neighbors are animals and trees
> Neighbors are mountains and grass
> Neighbors are all creatures on earth.

3. In attempting to develop a theology that includes nature and that recognizes the human place within it, some have used the phrase "creation-centered." I think this can be a very helpful phrase to name the kind of

theology we rightly seek in our ecological age. Christians such as Matthew Fox who employ the phrase "creation-centered" fittingly recognize that there is more to nature than what we call "life," at least inasmuch as "life" refers to the realms of plants and animals and perhaps also, as it does for me, to the living quality, the creativity, even within inorganic materials of the Earth. Nature also includes the cosmos, of whose evolutionary history we are a part. Used as Fox does (1983, 46), the phrase "creation-centered" can have the advantage of reminding us of this cosmic connection and of helping us to avoid a geocentrism, much less a biocentrism, that neglects cosmic awe. If a life-centered Christianity neglects such awe, it is insufficient.

Nevertheless the phrase "life-centered" can have advantages over "creation-centered." In the first place, the phrase "creation-centered" can suggest as its corollary the image of an external creator who creates the world out of nothing and who owns the created order as an artisan owns artifacts. In this work I wish to avoid such images of God. In the second place, the phrase "life-centered" has the advantage of highlighting the focus of our ethical concerns. Even as we are rightly awed by the larger cosmic context from which we have emerged, our center of ethical concern belongs to other living beings on Earth, not to stars and planets beyond us. At least at present we cannot assist in the renewal of stars and planets, much as we might feel deeply connected with them. We are not even sure they need renewal. But we can assist in the renewal of terrestrial life; we must assist in the elimination of the oppression of people, other animals, and the Earth. I use the phrase "life-centered" to make this clear.

Still others have preferred the phrase "God-centered" to "life-centered," or "theocentric" to "biocentric." In *Ethics from a Theocentric Perspective* (1981, 1984), for example, James Gustafson has chosen the phrase "theocentric" to name his own antidote to that anthropocentrism which, from his perspective as well as my own, has wrongly infected so much ethical thinking in Christianity. While there are differences between Gustafson's approach and mine, centering around my emphasis on divine love and his on divine sovereignty, I agree with his insistence that Christian ethics take seriously "the place of human beings in a larger ordering of life in nature and in history" (1981, 92). With Gustafson I do not think that the ordering of nature provides norms by which to guide human life, but I do think the history of life on Earth provides a framework in terms of which to understand human life, including the human search for norms.

Certainly, given some understandings of the phrase "God-centered," there is much value in this suggestion. If to be a God-centered Christian is to be on the side of each and every living being, as I believe God is, then the phrase "God-centered" is fine. Understood in this way, to be centered in God is to be centered in the things for which God yearns: namely, the well-being of life. There is little problematic, and much that is good, in this meaning of "God-centered." Just as I want to align myself with much of what the creation-centered tradition has to say, I want to align myself with much of what Gustafson has to say. In aiming toward postanthropocentric perspectives, many metaphors and phrases are needed, not just those I choose.

Still, I choose to highlight the phrase "life-centered" over "God-centered" for two reasons. First, much more directly than "creation-centered," the phrase "God-centered" can suggest to the popular imagination—though for Gustafson it does not—fidelity to a vainglorious ruler who is cut off from the world, who arbitrarily demands worship and obedience for his own sake, and who is the sole possessor of value. The God whom I hope to describe is neither vain, nor arbitrarily demanding, nor the sole possessor of value. In choosing "life-centered" over "God-centered," I wish to avoid connotations of a patriarchal, monarchical God to whom Christians owe blind obedience.

Second, and in a more positive vein, the God whom I hope to describe is indeed living, the supreme instance of that creativity and sentience with which we associate the word "life." A Christianity that is centered in life can and should involve trust in an ultimate Life, God, who is on the side of each and every living being. I use the phrase "life-centered" because the phrase includes within its horizons each and every living being, on the one hand, and the divine Life on the other, each understood in intimate connection with the other.

4. Of course, I am by no means the first to be interested in showing God's care for the whole of creation. All who are interested in doing so are deeply indebted to Irenaeus, the later Augustine, Francis of Assisi, John Wesley; to the Orthodox tradition with its sacramental approach to nature; to more recent life-centered theologies emerging in Africa and Asia; to emerging environmental theologies in North America; and, as I stress in the final chapter of this work, to feminist theologies.

Nor am I the first to try to show God's love for nature by developing a "panentheistic" perspective. In addition to other process thinkers such as John B. Cobb, Jr., and Charles Birch, by whom I am deeply influenced, I am also helped by the panentheistic perspectives of Sallie McFague and Arthur Peacocke.

I am in smaller company, however, in that I take the individual animal, with its needs and goals, as a point of departure for my own panentheistic perspective. For some reason most Christians who have taken nature as a point of departure for thinking about God have focused on the big picture, on ecosystems and the like. Moreover, I take the question of animal pain seriously: a question that I think must be faced squarely if Christians are to speak credibly of God's love for nature.

Even in taking animal pain seriously, I am not entirely alone. A very few Christians have taken animal pain, particularly that which is not caused by human beings, with the seriousness it deserves. Some, like the English philosopher Peter Geach, have concluded that "The Creator's Mind . . .

seems to be characterized by mere indifference to the pain that the elaborate interlocking teleologies of life involve" and that God "does not share with his creatures ... the virtue of sympathy with physical suffering" (1988, 40). Others, C. S. Lewis and C. E. M. Joad for example (1988, 55–62), are not satisfied with this conclusion (see also Lewis 1988a, 1988b). I find myself in their camp.

So do other process thinkers, particularly Daniel Dombrowski (1988), who is himself deeply influenced by the pioneering work of Hartshorne (e.g., 1968; 1978, and, in an ornithological context, 1973). All process thinkers are indebted to Hartshorne both for stressing the importance of the nonhuman world and for developing what Dombrowski calls a "metaphysics of animal rights."

Chapter 1: A Life-centered God

1. There are at least two similarities between Peacocke and process theologians in addition to those noted in the text of this chapter. The first concerns their respective conceptions of science and theology. Both Peacocke and process theologians are critical realists, which is to say (1) that both believe that science and theology tell us something about reality as it exists independent of human observation, and (2) that the models used in science and theology are fallible pointers—subject to criticism and revision—rather than infallible guides. Both would agree with Whitehead, who said that while a person rightly tries to understand the nature of reality, "the merest hint of dogmatic certainty as to finality of statement is an exhibition of folly" (1978, xiv).

Amid their respective endorsements of critical realism, a difference emerges. Peacocke focuses on the concepts of science and theology as such, often bracketing ontological questions. As Robert Russell puts it, "Peacocke espouses a form of critical realist epistemology ... tending to downplay the ontological questions which underlie it" (1986, 1). By contrast, process thinkers focus on ontological issues themselves, albeit in a way that is open to criticism and revision. They utilize heavily the metaphysical perspective of Whitehead, involving as it does what Whitehead called a "likely story"—informed by religion and phenomenological analysis as well as science—concerning what reality is really like. In many instances, this difference between Peacocke and process theologians is merely apparent. For although ontological questions are downplayed in Peacocke, they are not entirely neglected. Peacocke does, after all, say things about what nature is like, and in so doing he espouses an implicit ontology. As should be apparent from the similarities noted, this implicit ontology is not all that different from the explicit ontology of process theology.

The second additional similarity lies in the fact that both stress the importance of a nonreductionistic science. In Peacocke's instance, the emphasis is on the nonreducibility of high-level concepts and theories (those dealing, for example, with the psychological states of a human being who is laughing) to low-level concepts and theories (those dealing, for example, with the subatomic neurological activities associated with that psychological state). Neurological concepts miss both the meaning and the character of the laughing. In the case of process theologies, the emphasis is on the realities to which the concepts refer. From a process perspective, there actually is—in the laugher herself—something "more" than the totality of subatomic neurological activities in interaction.

The "more" of which process thinkers speak is not a supernatural reality immune from physical or chemical causation. It is the sensation of laughing itself, which is a subjective event that emerges out of, and in so doing integrates, the neurological activities of the brain, into a single momentary gestalt. The laugher—as a psyche—*is* this momentary act of laughing, plus all the psychic acts that preceded it and all that will come after it. This momentary act is more than the totality of neurological events in interaction because it is a subjective synthesis of those events, invisible to the observer's eye yet constitutive at the moment of the laugher's own "mind" or "soul." Although it is shaped by brain chemistry, it also shapes brain chemistry. It influences the brain even as the brain influences it.

Peacocke may or may not disagree with process thinkers on the relation of mind (or mental states) to brain (or brain states). While he does not take a definitive stand on whether the mind is identical to, or different from, the brain, he is strongly inclined toward a brain-mind identity (1984, 74–75; 1979, 131). Where he definitely *does* disagree with process theology, however, is with the assumption held by process thinkers that the cellular and subcellular activities of the brain, too, either are or are aggregate expressions of momentary pulsations of subjective (creative and sentient) energy. He rejects the "panpsychism" of process theology, which is the view that all matter—inorganic as well as organic—has or is composed of actualities that have primitive degrees of inwardness. Peacocke's view is that this metaphysical hypothesis is unnecessary. Human (and other animal) subjectivity can well be explained as a phenomenon that emerged evolutionarily out of creative, though insentient, matter (1979, 125–127).

Process thinkers reject the emergent evolution model, at least as it applies to subjectivity. They recognize with Peacocke that many new structures of existence (protons, atoms, molecules, living cells) have entered the history of nature at various points in cosmic history and that these new structures have brought with them new properties. They know that when sodium and chlorine atoms first came together to make common salt, new qualities emerged in the compound sodium chloride that were not contained previously in the isolated atoms. But they argue that subjectivity is not an externally observed property like salinity. It is not an objective attribute among objective attributes. Rather, it is inwardness or sentience: the capacity consciously or nonconsciously to take into account something else from a subjective point of view. Such sentience is at the very heart of life as we know it, and it cannot be explained as a property that mysteriously emerges out of material entities totally lacking such sentience. Instead we must recognize (as certain religious traditions have long known, and as quantum mechanics itself can imply) that there are degrees of conscious or nonconscious inwardness throughout matter and that the sentience of living beings is an expression of, rather than an exception to, the inchoate sentience of inorganic matter. This means that, if by "life" we mean inwardness, allegedly dead matter is not utterly dead; it is just much less alive. And it means that, as applied to subjectivity, an emergent evolution model wrongly leaves the mechanistic model of matter unchallenged at the level of inorganic matter, when that model itself deserves to be challenged.

However this debate is resolved, what is clear is that for both, even amid this fundamental difference, science cannot and should not be reductionistic. The concepts of biology cannot be reduced to those of physics, nor can those of psychology be reduced to those of biology. For both, new structures and new forms of existence have evolved that cannot be reduced to mere aggregates of simpler forms. Process thinkers would argue that these new structures are new forms of sentience; Peacocke would argue that sentience is itself a new form.

2. One approach "is based on the analogy of human personal action in the world as elaborated by the philosophy of action" (O. Thomas 1983, 231). A second—which presents insuperable problems for theodicy—is "the traditional approach" in which "God as primary cause acts in and through all secondary causes in nature and history" (1983, 232). A third approach emphasizes that science on the one hand and faith in God's providential activity on the other are "two different ways of looking at natural historical process" from different, though complementary, points of view (1983, 232). A fourth is that of process theology, which suggests that God is an actual influence among influences in natural processes.

Chapter 2: A Life-centered Ethic

1. Even among those who do not agree with Leopold concerning the inadequacies of traditional Western ethics, as in the case of John Passmore (1974), the first modern philosopher to write a systematic treatise in environmental philosophy, Leopold's arguments serve as a standard requiring response.

2. The cells in the dog's body, too, might be monarchies, albeit of a primitive kind because of the simpler nature of a cell's nervous system. Amid their complexity they exhibit a capacity for unified response suggesting that they have reality for themselves as well as reality for others. They too have some degree of intrinsic value as psyches. A dog is a monarchy of monarchies. Indeed, even the organelles within these cells might be monarchies, for they too exhibit a capacity for unified response that suggests subjective unity in its own right. But here monarchical forms of organiza-

tion probably stop. The molecules of which these organelles are composed are probably democracies, as are the atoms composing these molecules, for molecules and atoms seem to lack subjective centers, even though the energy events composing them exhibit small degrees of subjective responsiveness. As a psychophysical organism, then, the dog can be conceived as a monarchy of cellular monarchies, each of which are themselves monarchies of organellic monarchies, which are themselves monarchies of democratically organized subcellular parts.

Chapter 4: A Postpatriarchal Christianity

1. In identifying these two aspects I diverge slightly from Brock's treatment of erotic power. Whereas she defines erotic power as "the power of our primal interrelatedness" (1988, 26), emphasizing erotic power as something that lies between selves and is in some sense more than each self, I approach it from the point of view of an individual self or, to use her term, "heart," who has already been shaped by the power of relationships and who, in the immediacy of a new moment, is aware of and influenced by other people and the world. These approaches are, I hope, complementary; in any case there is truth in both of them.

2. I owe to my colleague Jon Guthrie, Campus Counselor and Chaplain at Hendrix College, the insight that incompleteness, not death, is that which appropriately elicits a hope for life after death.

Works Cited

Abe, Masao. 1985. *Zen and Western Thought.* Ed. William R. LaFleur. Honolulu: University of Hawaii Press.

Berry, Thomas. 1987. "The Earth: A New Context for Religious Unity." In *Thomas Berry and the New Cosmology.* Ed. Anne Lonergan and Caroline Richards. Mystic, Conn.: Twenty-Third Publications, 27–39.

———. 1988. *The Dream of the Earth.* San Francisco: Sierra Club Books.

Birch, L. Charles. 1966. *Nature and God.* Philadelphia: Westminster Press.

———. 1987. "Chance and Purpose in Evolution." Unpublished essay written for the consultation on "Nature and God" of the World Council of Churches at Glion, Switzerland, September 6–12, 1987.

Birch, Charles, and John B. Cobb, Jr. 1981. *The Liberation of Life: From Cell to Community.* Cambridge: Cambridge University Press.

Blackstone, William. 1980. "The Search for an Environmental Ethic." In *Matters of Life and Death: New Introductory Essays in Moral Philosophy.* Ed. Tom Regan. New York: Random House, 299–335.

Bohm, David. 1980. *Wholeness and the Implicate Order.* London: Routledge & Kegan Paul.

Brock, Rita Nakashima. 1988. *Journeys by Heart: A Christology of Erotic Power.* New York: Crossroad Publishing Co.

Brueggemann, Walter. 1978. *The Prophetic Imagination.* Philadelphia: Fortress Press.

Buber, Martin. 1960. "Spinoza, Sabbatai Zvi, and the Baal-Shem." In *The Origin and Meaning of Hasidi.* Ed. Maurice Friedman. New York: Horizon Press.

Callicott, J. Baird. 1980. "Animal Liberation: A Triangular Affair." *Environmental Ethics* 2(4):311–338.

———. 1988. "Animal Liberation and Environmental Ethics: Back Together Again." In *In Defense of the Land Ethic: Essays in Environmental Philosophy.* Albany, N.Y.: State University of New York Press, 115–174.

Carson, Rachel. 1970. *Silent Spring.* New York: Fawcett Publications.

Chodorow, Nancy. 1978. *The Reproduction of Mothering: Psychological*

Theory and Women's Development. Berkeley, Calif.: University of California Press.

Cobb, John B., Jr., 1965. *A Christian Natural Theology: Based on the Thought of Alfred North Whitehead.* Philadelphia: Westminster Press.

———. 1969. *God and the World.* Philadelphia: Westminster Press.

———. 1975. *Christ in a Pluralistic Age.* Philadelphia: Westminster Press.

———. 1977. "Buddhist Emptiness and the Christian God." *Journal of the American Academy of Religion* 45 (March):11–25.

———. 1982. *Beyond Dialogue: Toward a Mutual Transformation of Christianity and Buddhism.* Philadelphia: Fortress Press.

Cobb, John B., Jr., and David Ray Griffin. 1976. *Process Theology: An Introductory Exposition.* Philadelphia: Westminster Press.

Daly, Mary. 1975. *The Church and the Second Sex: With a New Feminist Postchristian Introduction by the Author.* San Francisco: Harper & Row.

———. 1978. *Gyn/Ecology: The Metaethics of Radical Feminism.* Boston: Beacon Press.

Davaney, Sheila Greeve, ed. 1981. "Introduction." *Feminism and Process Thought: The Harvard Divinity School/Claremont Center for Process Studies Symposium Papers.* Lewiston, N.Y.: Edwin Mellen Press, 1–9.

Day, David. 1981. *The Doomsday Book of Animals: A Natural History of Vanished Species.* New York: Viking Press.

Devall, Bill, and George Sessions. 1985. *Deep Ecology.* Layton, Utah: Peregrine Smith Books.

Dombrowski, Daniel A. 1988. *Hartshorne and the Metaphysics of Animal Rights.* Albany, N.Y.: State University of New York Press.

Dunfee, Sue. 1982. "The Sin of Hiding: A Feminist Critique of Reinhold Niebuhr's Account of the Sin of Pride." *Soundings* Fall:316–327.

Durell, Lee. 1986. *State of the Ark: An Atlas of Conservation in Action.* New York: Doubleday & Co.

Ehrlich, Paul, and Anne Ehrlich. 1981. *Extinction: The Causes and Consequences of the Disappearance of Species.* New York: Random House.

Fiorenza, Elisabeth Schüssler. 1983. *In Memory of Her: A Feminist Reconstruction of Christian Origins.* New York: Crossroad Publishing Co.

Fox, Matthew. 1983. *Original Blessing.* Santa Fe, N. Mex.: Bear & Co.

Geach, Peter. "Divine Indifference." *See* Linzey 1988, 52–55.

Granberg-Michaelson, Wesley. 1984. *A Worldly Spirituality: The Call to Take Care of the Earth.* San Francisco: Harper & Row.

Gray, Elizabeth Dodson. 1979. *Green Paradise Lost.* Wellesley, Mass.: Roundtable Press.

Griffin, David, ed. 1987a. "Introduction." *Physics and the Ultimate Significance of Time: Bohm, Prigogine, and Process Philosophy.* Albany, N.Y.: State University of New York Press, 1–48.

———. 1987b. "Report on the Conference 'Toward a Post-Modern World.' " *Center for Process Studies Newsletter* 11(1):5–12.

————. 1988. "Introduction: The Reenchantment of Science." *The Reenchantment of Science.* Albany, N.Y.: State University of New York Press, 1–31.

Griffin, Donald. 1984. *Animal Thinking.* Cambridge, Mass.: Harvard University Press.

Griffin, Susan. 1979. *Woman and Nature: The Roaring Inside Her.* New York: Harper & Row.

Gustafson, James M. 1981. *Ethics from a Theocentric Perspective, Vol. 1: Theology and Ethics.* Chicago: University of Chicago Press.

————. 1984. *Ethics from a Theocentric Perspective, Vol. 2: Ethics and Theology.* Chicago: University of Chicago Press.

Hall, Douglas John. 1986. *Imaging God: Dominion as Stewardship.* Grand Rapids: Wm. B. Eerdmans Publishing Co.

Harper's Bible Dictionary. 1985. Ed. Paul J. Achtemeier. San Francisco: Harper & Row.

Hartshorne, Charles. 1968. *Beyond Humanism.* Lincoln, Nebr.: University of Nebraska Press.

————. 1973. *Born to Sing.* Bloomington, Ind.: Indiana University Press.

————. 1978. "Foundations for a Humane Ethics: What Human Beings Have in Common with Other Higher Animals." *See* Morris and Fox 1978, 159–172.

Heaney, John J. 1984. *The Sacred and the Psychic: Parapsychology and Christian Theology.* Ramsey, N.J.: Paulist Press.

Heidegger, Martin. 1977. "Building Dwelling Thinking." In *Martin Heidegger: Basic Writings.* Ed. David Farrell Krell. New York: Harper & Row, 323–339.

Heschel, Abraham J. 1965. *The Prophets: An Introduction.* San Francisco: Harper & Row.

Hick, John. 1988. *See* Linzey 1988, 62–66.

Howell, Nancy. 1988. "The Promise of a Process Feminist Theory of Relations." *Process Studies* 17(2):78–87.

Jantzen, Grace. 1984. *God's World, God's Body.* Philadelphia: Westminster Press.

Joad, C. E. M., with C. S. Lewis. 1988. "The Pains of Animals." *See* Linzey 1988, 55–62.

Joranson, Philip N., and Ken Butigan. 1984. *Cry of the Environment: Rebuilding the Christian Creation Tradition.* Santa Fe, N. Mex.: Bear & Co.

Keller, Catherine. 1986. *From a Broken Web: Separation, Sexism, and Self.* Boston: Beacon Press.

Keller, Evelyn Fox. 1983. *A Feeling for the Organism: The Life and Work of Barbara McClintock.* San Francisco: W. H. Freeman and Co.

Lambert, Jean. 1981. "Becoming Human: A Contextual Approach to Decisions About Pregnancy and Abortion." *See* Davaney 1981, 106–136.

Leopold, Aldo. 1949. *A Sand County Almanac.* New York: Oxford University Press.

Lewis, C. S. 1988a. "Animal Resurrection." *See* Linzey 1988, 107–109.

———. 1988b. "A Case for Abolition." *See* Linzey 1988, 160–164.

Linzey, Andrew. 1986. "Animals." *The Westminster Dictionary of Christian Ethics.* Ed. James F. Childress and John Macquarrie. Philadelphia: Westminster Press, 28–33.

———. 1987. *Christianity and the Rights of Animals.* New York: Crossroad Publishing Co.

———. 1988. *Animals and Christianity: A Book of Readings.* New York: Crossroad Publishing Co.

Livezey, Lois G. "Women, Power, and Politics: Feminist Theology in Process Perspective." *Process Studies* 17(2):67–77.

McDaniel, Jay. 1975. "Introduction: Conference on Mahayana Buddhism and Whitehead." With John B. Cobb, Jr. *Philosophy East and West* 25:393–413.

———. 1983. "Physical Matter as Creative and Sentient." *Environmental Ethics* 5(4):291–317.

———. 1984a. "Mahayana Enlightenment in Process Perspective." In *Buddhism and American Thinkers.* Ed. Kenneth K. Inada and Nolan P. Jacobson. Albany, N.Y.: State University of New York Press, 51–69.

———. 1984b. "Zen Buddhism and Prophetic Christianity." *Encounter* 45(4):303–323.

———. 1985. "The God of the Oppressed and the God Who Is Empty." *Journal of Ecumenical Studies* 22(4):687–402.

———. 1986. "A Feeling for the Organism: Christian Spirituality as Openness to Fellow Creatures." *Environmental Ethics* 8 (Spring):33–46.

McFague, Sallie. 1987. *Models of God: Theology for an Ecological, Nuclear Age.* Philadelphia: Fortress Press.

Merchant, Carolyn. 1985. *The Death of Nature: Women, Ecology, and the Scientific Revolution.* San Francisco: Harper & Row.

Moltmann, Jürgen. 1974. *The Crucified God.* Trans. R. A. Wilson and J. Bowden. London: SCM Press.

———. 1988. "Land Ethics, Animal Rights, and Process Theology." *Process Studies* 17(2):88–102.

———. 1985. *God in Creation: A New Theology of Creation and the Spirit of God.* Trans. Margaret Kohl. San Francisco: Harper & Row.

Moran, Gabriel. 1987. "Dominion Over the Earth." *Commonweal* 114(21):697–701.

Morris, Richard Knowles, and Michael W. Fox, eds. 1978. *On the Fifth Day: Animal Rights and Human Ethics.* Washington, D.C.: Acropolis Books.

Muray, Leslie A. 1988. *An Introduction to the Process Understanding of Science, Society and the Self: A Philosophy for Modern Humanity.* Lewiston, N.Y.: Edwin Mellen Press.

Myers, Norman. 1986. "The Environmental Crisis: How Big, How Important?" *Report and Background Papers of the Meeting of the Working Group, GDR, July.* Geneva: WCC Publs., pp. 101–114.

Nobuhara, Tokiyuki. 1983. "Interpreting Christ/Buddha." *Buddhist-Christian Studies* 3:63–97.

Noddings, Nel. 1984. *Caring: A Feminine Approach to Ethics and Moral Education.* Berkeley, Calif.: University of California Press.

Oxford English Dictionary. 1970. Vol. V. Oxford: Clarendon Press.

Partnow, Elaine, ed. 1977. *The Quotable Woman: Volume Two, 1900–the Present.* Los Angeles: Pinnacle Books.

Parvey, Constance. 1984. "Re-membering: A Global Perspective on Women." In *Christian Feminism: Visions of a New Humanity.* Ed. Judith L. Weidman. San Francisco: Harper & Row, 158–179.

Passmore, John. 1974. *Man's Responsibility for Nature.* London: Gerald Duckworth & Co.

Peacocke, Arthur R. 1974. *Science and the Christian Experiment.* London: Oxford University Press.

———. 1979. *Creation and the World of Science: The Bampton Lectures, 1978.* Oxford: Clarendon Press.

———. 1984. *Intimations of Reality: Critical Realism in Science and Religion.* Notre Dame, Ind.: University of Notre Dame Press.

———. 1986. *God and the New Biology.* San Francisco: Harper & Row.

Plaskow, Judith. 1980. *Sex, Sin, and Grace: Women's Experience and the Theologies of Reinhold Niebuhr and Paul Tillich.* Washington, D.C.: University Press of America.

Prigogine, Ilya, and Isabelle Stengers. 1984. *Order Out of Chaos: Man's New Dialogue with Nature.* New York: Bantam Books.

Regan, Tom. 1983. *The Case for Animal Rights.* Berkeley, Calif.: University of California Press.

———, ed. 1986. *Animal Sacrifices: Religious Perspectives on the Use of Animals in Science.* Philadelphia: Temple University Press.

Robbins, John. 1987. *Diet for a New America.* Walpole, N.H.: Stillpoint Publishing.

Rollin, Bernard E. 1981. *Animal Rights and Human Morality.* Buffalo, N.Y.: Prometheus Books.

Rolston, Holmes, III. 1981. "Values in Nature." *Environmental Ethics* 3(2):113–128.

———. 1982. "Are Values in Nature Subjective or Objective?" *Environmental Ethics* 4(1):125–151.

———. 1986. *Philosophy Gone Wild: Essays in Environmental Ethics.* Buffalo, N.Y.: Prometheus Books.

———. 1987. *Science and Religion: A Critical Survey.* New York: Random House.

———. 1988. *Environmental Ethics: Duties to and Values in the Natural World.* Philadelphia: Temple University Press.

Ruether, Rosemary Radford. 1975. *New Woman, New Earth.* New York: Seabury Press.

――――. 1983. *Sexism and God-Talk: Toward a Feminist Theology.* Boston: Beacon Press.

Russell, Letty M., et al. 1988. *Inheriting Our Mothers' Gardens: Feminist Theology in Third World Perspective.* Philadelphia, Pa.: Westminster Press.

Russell, R. J. 1986. "Crossing Between Physics and Theology: Reliable Bridge or Slippery Leap?" Unpublished paper presented at Annual Meeting of the American Academy of Religion, Atlanta, Georgia.

Ryder, Richard. 1975. *Victims of Science.* London: Davis-Poynter.

――――. 1985. "Speciesism in the Laboratory." In *In Defense of Animals.* Ed. Peter Singer. San Francisco: Harper & Row, 77–88.

Saiving, Valerie. 1979. "The Human Situation: A Feminine View." In *Womanspirit Rising: A Feminist Reader in Religion.* Ed. Carol Christ and Judith Plaskow. San Francisco: Harper & Row, 25–42.

Santmire, H. Paul. 1985. *The Travail of Nature: The Ambiguous Ecological Promise of Christian Theology.* Philadelphia: Fortress Press.

Singer, Peter. 1975. *Animal Liberation: A New Ethics for Our Treatment of Animals.* New York: Avon Books.

Smith, Huston. 1958. *The Religions of Man.* San Francisco: Harper & Row.

Soelle, Dorothee. 1975. *Suffering.* Philadelphia: Fortress Press.

――――. 1984. *To Work and to Love.* Philadelphia: Fortress Press.

Stapp, Henry Pierce. 1977. "Quantum Mechanics, Local Causality, and Process Philosophy." *Process Studies* 7:174.

Suchocki, Marjorie Hewitt. 1982. *God-Christ-Church: A Practical Guide to Process Theology.* New York: Crossroad Publishing Co.

Suzuki, Daisetzu. 1973. *Zen and Japanese Culture.* Princeton, N.J.: Princeton University Press.

Thomas, Lewis. 1974. *The Lives of a Cell: Notes of a Biology Watcher.* New York: Viking Press.

Thomas, Owen, ed. 1983. *God's Activity in the World: The Contemporary Problem.* Chico, Calif.: Scholars Press.

Tripp, Rhoda Thomas, comp. 1987. *The International Thesaurus of Quotations.* New York: Harper & Row.

Walker, Alice. 1982. *The Color Purple.* New York: Washington Square Press.

Ward, Keith. 1988. "Sentient Afterlife." *See* Linzey 1988, 104–105.

Warren, Karen. 1987. "Feminism and Ecology: Making Connections." *Environmental Ethics* 9:3–20.

Warren, Mary Ann. 1983. "Rights of the Nonhuman World." In *Environmental Philosophy.* Ed. Robert Elliot and Arran Gare. University Park, Pa.: State University of Pennsylvania Press, 109–134.

Washbourn, Penelope. 1981. "The Dynamics of Female Experience: Process Models and Human Values." *See* Davaney 1981, 83–105.

Wesley, John. 1988. "The General Deliverance." *See* Linzey 1988, 101–103.

Wheeler, Barbara H. 1981. "Accountability to Women in Theological Seminaries." *Religious Education* 76 (July–Aug.):382–390.

Whitehead, Alfred North. 1933. *Adventures of Ideas.* New York: Macmillan Co.

———. 1978. *Process and Reality,* corrected ed. Ed. David Ray Griffin and Donald W. Sherburne. New York: Free Press.

Wiesel, Elie. 1960. *Night.* Trans. Stella Roday. New York: Hill & Wang.

———. 1981. *Five Biblical Portraits.* Notre Dame, Ind.: University of Notre Dame Press.

World Commission on Environment and Development. 1987. *Our Common Future.* New York: Oxford University Press.

World Resources Institute. 1988. *World Resources 1988–89: An Assessment of the Resource Base That Supports the Global Economy.* New York: Basic Books.

Zimmerman, Michael E. 1987. "Feminism, Deep Ecology, and Environmental Ethics." *Environmental Ethics* 9:21–44.

Index